IT'S ALL
ROCK-N-ROLL
TO ME

Profiling Today's Popular artists and bands From a Biblical Perspective

by David S. Hart

Published by New Song Publishers, © 1996

"It's All Rock-N-Roll to Me: Profiling Today's Popular Artists and Bands From a Biblical Perspective"

By David S. Hart

Published by New Song Publishing, a division of Al Menconi Ministries, PO Box 5008, San Marcos, CA 92069-1050

ISBN 0-942925-08-4

Printed in the United States of America.

TABLE OF CONTENTS

DEDICATION

This book is dedicated to my wife, the Lovely Velva, my jewel. She brings me balance and helps me find the peaceful center in my life. She is the clearest measure of what it means to be loved by Jesus Christ that I've ever known.

ACKNOWLEDGMENTS

I want to acknowledge the ministry of Al Menconi Ministries, without which this book would not be possible. The information and experience I've gained there has had a most profound impact on me and the ministry I have today. I want to thank Al Menconi for his advice and direction in shaping the book and Mike Atkinson for his meticulous attention to detail—a rare and invaluable gift for this kind of work. I want to thank the staff at Al Menconi Ministries for putting up with my "artistic temperament"—Melody, Stephanie, Jennifer, Richard and Ray. Last but not least, I'm more than grateful to Wayno, who did so much detail work for me, combing the files for just the right article, fact, or photo. Thank you, my friend.

I also want to acknowledge the lambs and lions of my church, Sanctuary, San Diego. They are the ones who inspire me to drive deep into the darkest realms of rock-n-roll to learn what I can to reach this generation for Christ. Most of the time, I think I learn more from them than I teach. To Steve and April Gray—thanks for helping me make the vision real. To Ed and Cynthia Carter—thank you for giving Sanctuary a renewed vision and direction. To Wayno—thank you for the long talks and the faithful friendship, you have been a good student. To Robert— thanks for teaching me about the music. To Kip—thanks for teaching me about rave. To Dawn, Kathleen, Stacey, Dianne, Rebecca, Karelyn, Brian, Larry and Kristen, and Mark and Kristy—your support gave me the freedom to finish this book. To Chrissie, Shanna, Sean, Ryan, Mark, Auggie, and Sherryl and Kevin—you are my reward. Thank you for letting me be your pastor and your friend.

Finally, thanks be to my Lord and Savior, Jesus Christ, who gave me a head for trivia, a heart for kids, and the gift of eternal life.

FORWARD

I have to admit that I'm not a big fan of rock music. I think I lost interest when Creedence Clearwater Revival broke up. My ears are simply no match for those 500-watt amplifiers they use these days. And on top of that, I play banjo in a bluegrass band!

I am, however, a big fan of kids. I like to be with teenagers. I've been in youth work for more than 30 years, and I'm also the parent of three kids who are very fond of music that is, well, much too loud.

So even though I don't listen to rock-n-roll, I am well aware that the kids I care about do, and that makes it important to me. I try to at least be conversant in rock. I can actually speak rock-ese a little bit. Thanks to people like Dave Hart and Al Menconi, I think I know the difference between grunge and hip-hop. Ask me sometime.

But wait a minute. Why would a 50-year-old bluegrass music nut even *want* to know about that other music. The answer probably has something to do with why God chose to enter the world of human beings some 2000 years ago in the person of His Son, Jesus Christ. Jesus forsook the beautiful music of the heavenlies to become a man and endure the music of sinful humanity. He couldn't save us from a distance and he didn't.

In the same way, we who do youth work believe in *incarnational* youth ministry. That means we believe it is important to enter the world of today's youth and try to speak their language. Otherwise they won't hear what we have to say.

I really admire people like Dave and Al. Hey, they are starting to get old, too! (Sorry, guys.) Their ears probably hurt just as much as mine do when those bands crank up the volume. But they are obedient servants, following the pattern of Jesus by entering the world of young people and attempting to understand what's being communicated in their culture.

They believe, as I do, that the best hope for today's kids are adults who are willing to come along side them, to mentor them, and to engage them in dialogue. We can help kids tremendously and influence them to become life-long followers of Jesus by taking them and their world seriously. But we can't do that by remaining aloof. We can't do it from a distance. We must show kids that we are interested in their world, and one good way to do that is to pay attention to the music they enjoy.

Many people today lament the "power" of rock music over our kids. Some like to blame the music for all sorts of problems and attitudes that are so evident in today's youth culture. But if rock music and other forms of entertainment have any power at all, it is power by default. It only fills the void left by the absence of significant adults in their lives.

When young people have parents who are there for them, as well as other caring adults who are willing to offer guidance and direction, then there is no need to worry much about the influence of pop culture. My kids listen to rock music (they hate bluegrass), and they have learned to sort out the good from the bad, the true from the false, the right from the wrong. As a parent, the best I can hope for is the knowledge that my kids have learned how to think and how to make good decisions about their listening and watching habits.

That's what this book is all about. It is not a weapon to use against kids, but a tool to help parents and other adults understand the world of youth a little better. Dave Hart has really done his homework. He has provided all of us with a guide to the music of today's youth (and even some clues about the music of my younger days), so that we can discuss the real issues with them, which of course has little to do with the beat or the volume.

Kids won't listen to us when we simply criticize and scold. But when we listen to them — and their culture — they become much more receptive to the guidance and direction that we offer. Flip through the pages that follow, and it will become obvious that *It's All Rock-n-Roll To Me* is a labor of love — a huge undertaking by someone who not only loves music, but loves young people and loves Jesus Christ. This is a book that every parent and youth worker should have. I highly recommend this book to anyone who wants to make a difference in the lives of kids.

Wayne Rice
Co-founder, Youth Specialties
Director, Understanding Your Teenager Seminars

INTRODUCTION

"It's all rock-n-roll to me!" I can't tell you the number of times Al Menconi and I have heard comments like that. Most of the Christian parents we talk to admit they wouldn't know the difference between a White Zombie and a White Christmas! Kids don't care if it's rock or rap, secular or Christian. What's the difference? As long as it sounds good, it's all rock-n-roll to them!

But today's music shouldn't be so easily dismissed by Christians. It invades every portion of our lives and affects every aspect of our being: body, heart, mind, soul, and spirit. Anything with this much potential power in our lives should be examined more carefully for its spiritual impact. After all, the Bible says we are to take *every* thought captive to the obedience of Jesus Christ (2 Cor. 10:5).

This book is an attempt to help you do that. It's for parents who feel out of touch. It's for youth workers and church leaders who have run out of time. And it's for music fans, who feel so in tune, they rarely take the time to really think about the music they listen to.

So please start by taking the time to read the Forward, because Wayne Rice has completely captured the real purpose and intent of this book. It is **not** simply a list of the most satanic bands we could find. It doesn't reject every artist simply because they're secular—there are positive things to be said about many artists. Nor is it an exhaustive list of every artist who's had a fleeting moment in music history.

It **is** an attempt to offer an organized set of profiles that is interesting and informative, without being too superficial or too complex. These are the bands parents and teens keep asking us about at our seminars. These are the groups that are making the news. These are the groups we've had to wrestle with personally. These are the artists and bands we feel we really have something to say about.

You may find that your favorite artist is missing. It's impossible to profile every artist who's ever had a hit. However, we have tried to offer several profiles for most styles of popular music. If you don't find your favorite artist here, read the profiles on those groups that are similar to the one you're looking for and apply the analysis to your favorite group. We also recommend that you write us about any artist or group we may have missed. Tell us why they are important to you, and we'll try to include them in a future edition.

We want this to be an educational primer for those who are not well-acquainted with today's music. We also hope that even the most knowledgeable rock music fan will discover some unique facts and information they'd never known before. Mostly we hope that everyone who reads this book will start seeing secular music through God's eyes, instead of the world's.

This book offers some valuable *facts* to help you make more spiritual choices about today's music. But you also need to understand the *philosophy* of dealing with this subject. I encourage you to read the articles "Why They Listen" (page 149) and "The Four Philosophies (of Rock Music)" (page 150).

Al Menconi and I have also written the book *Staying In Tune: A Rational Response To Your Child's Music* (Standard Publishers) to give you a more in-depth look at this topic. A complete look at the process of handling rock music in the home can be found in Al Menconi's book, *Ten Steps To Talk to Your Kids About Values*. Al Menconi Ministries also offers a bi-monthly magazine called *Media Update* which will keep you up-to-date on the world of music and entertainment. (For a free sample of *Media Update*, simply call **1-800-78MUSIC**.) You can find out more about any of these resources by contacting us at Al Menconi Ministries, P.O. Box 5008, San Marcos, CA 92069, or by calling 1-619-591-4696. Finally, if you are looking for profiles on the latest bands not yet included in this book, you can call our info line at **1-900-872-1717**.

Finally, before you plunge into the profiles, let me offer a warning to parents and a caution to the kids:

A Warning to Parents: Some of the material quoted in this book is somewhat crude and worldly. Some will find these reports too graphic for their tastes and experience, and they may be doing their children a disservice exposing them to such material. If you have been successful in insulating your children from the world of TV, movies, and rock music, you probably don't need this book in the first place. Sadly, however, many Christian children today have been exposed to far worse than what we're reporting here.

It is not our intention to offend Christians or to over-sensationalize this material. We do not wish to glorify these groups or their behavior, but it is important that somebody expose them to the light of conviction (Eph. 5:6-16). Our reports remain relatively tame compared to some of the things these artists are actually saying and singing to our children. However, it is impossible to give you an accurate description of the ungodly lengths some of these groups have gone to without relating some of this graphic material. Instead of being offended at us for reporting it, we hope you will be convicted about the depths of sin some of these groups have fallen into.

Finally, let me warn you that there is another reason this book may be hard for some of you to read. Aside from the issue of abortion, there are few topics that get people as emotionally wound up as music. Everyone has their own idea of what good music is, and what they think of people who disagree with them. So this book will undoubtedly stir up some strong opinions and emotions. Some readers will feel that I've been too positive and too easy on some of these music groups. Many fans will feel that I've been too hard and judgmental on their favorite artists. I've tried to remain factual and biblical in my analysis, but I'm sure that my emotions have occasionally gotten in the way, as well. Having been warned, however, I trust that most of you can recognize your feelings for what they are, and go on to look for God's perspective in these matters.

A Caution to Young Rock Fans: A lot of adults, especially Christian adults, have a lot to say about today's music. Some of it is just their opinion, some of it comes from books. When you study those books, they seem to be written by old people who have been locked up in some church tower for fifty years. They're overreacting to some gross album covers, and they don't seem to know what's really going on in the music scene today. I realize that it's going to be tempting to dismiss me as just another "gray-haired old guy" who doesn't really know what he's talking about. Please don't do that. Let me tell you why.

1) *I don't hate rock-n-roll.* I'm actually not *that* old. I'm old enough to remember the '60s: the Beatles, Jimi Hendrix, Janis Joplin. But I'm not old enough to think that organ music is better than rock-n-roll. Like Larry Norman, I always wondered why the devil should have all the good music. I *like* music, and my tastes run from classical to jazz, and from Celtic folk to heavy metal. I like it so much, I actually promoted Christian concerts for several years. I worked behind the scenes with everyone from Amy Grant to Stryper. I'm proud to say that I worked in the early days with metal bands like Bloodgood, Deliverance, Rez, and Whitecross; as well as early punk groups like Undercover, the Altar Boys, and One Bad Pig. I remain friends with many of these artists today. I like rock-n-roll and I'm not bothered by a good beat or cranking up the volume.

2) *I don't hate kids.* I've spent the better part of my life learning to work with youth. I majored in youth work at seminary. I got training in drug and alcohol counseling and worked on suicide hotlines, so I'd be better prepared to help young people who were struggling with those issues. I was a church youth worker for a number of years. God led me to start the Sanctuary church in San Diego, because He knew that some kids didn't fit in the traditional church and needed a "rock-n-roll refuge" to find Him. When we started years ago, we primarily reached out to the heavy metal arena. Today the church ministers to the gothic, industrial, and alternative underground.

The point is that I've spent years learning how to relate to teens. I care about you and I care about the world you're growing up in. I know that when someone is critical of your favorite music, it feels like they are being critical of you. This book is not an attempt to attack you or the fact that you like this music. But I'm not convinced all this music is all that good for you. Those guys on the radio are not all telling you the truth. They don't all have your best interests at heart. When I see them glorifying your pain and self-destruction, it bothers me. That's when I feel I need to take a stand and say, "Look beyond the beat. What are these guys really saying? Do you really want that in your life?"

3) *I do my homework.* Take time to really read these profiles. You may not agree with all of my conclusions, but I think you'll agree that I've done my homework. I've been doing research on music for Al Menconi Ministries for over twelve years now. I'm one of the few guys you'll ever meet who actually gets *paid* to watch MTV! I read dozens of rock magazines every month. I've read dozens of books and watched hours of videos on the history of rock music. The ministry has several filing cabinets full of information on bands and artists, and I've combed through hundreds of files to learn more about these bands.

But I haven't limited my studies to some musty office. I spend lots of time with real rock fans every week. And I ask a lot of questions to learn from them—who are the hot new groups, what do they sound like, what are their lyrics about, what's cool about them, why do you like them?

I also take every opportunity to meet and talk with secular artists when the occasion arises. When Al Menconi was invited to participate in a debate about censorship, we had a good talk with Jello Biafra of the Dead Kennedys (we found him to be intelligent, witty, articulate, and sadly mistaken about Christianity). Al and I also debated Frank Zappa at Cal State, Fullerton on censorship (he ignored our arguments and claimed the PMRC (the Parents' Music Resource Center) was just a ploy to help Al Gore run for President). I've debated the merits of rap music with Ice-T's manager, and met with the manager of Gwar, who was surprised that a Christian even knew who they were. Al and I were consulted for both the Ozzy Osbourne and the Judas Priest trials, when the parents claimed that music caused their children's suicides.

I once performed a wedding for a rock-n-roll friend of mine and had an interesting talk with his best man, Lemmy Kilmister of Motorhead. Al and I have had a running dialogue for several years with Bob Guccione, Jr., the editor of *SPIN* magazine, and I've done extensive interviews with artists like King's X, Maria McKee of Lone Justice, and Eva O (formerly of the punk band Christian Death) for magazine articles. My most interesting, and perhaps most dangerous, was a confrontation with Glenn Benton of the death metal band Deicide outside a club where he was performing in San Diego.

I'm not telling you all this just to try to make you think I'm so cool. I'm sharing this so you'll understand that I haven't been stuck in some holy tower, oblivious to the real world. I've been out in the real music world, too. So as you read these profiles, you are free to disagree with me, but don't dismiss me as some old fuddy-duddy with his head stuck in the sand. I really make the effort to stay in touch with my topic, and I think that will become obvious as you read this book.

Guidelines for the Reader

1) The artists profiled in this book are organized in alphabetical order, not by style or type of music (which is described within the profile itself).

2) Throughout the book, you will find references to other bands or artists. If their name is highlighted in **bold print,** it indicates that they have their own profile in the book. (Don't forget to look them up and study them, as well.) *Album Titles* are placed in italics (usually followed by the year of the album's release), while "Song Titles" are placed in quotes. When cited, "*song lyrics are found in italics and quotes.*"

3) Each artist profile is followed by a section called the *Music Exchange.* In it we offer one or more Christian music artists or groups who might appeal to the fan of the mainstream artist in the profile. While some of these artists are no longer recording, as with secular music, their fans still listen to them and their music can still be found if you dig a little. Most of this music is available in Christian bookstores, some mainstream music stores, or through mail-order services (e.g., *True Tunes* or Long's). We suggest you exchange as much music for these Christian groups as possible. It's easier to remove unhealthy, secular music from your children's grasp, if you offer them something in its place—something that focuses on a spiritual point of view in a musical style they can enjoy and understand. But there are some cautions:

-Just because a group is listed in the *Music Exchange,* does not mean that it sounds *exactly* like the group in the profile. Please don't offer your child a Christian group and tell them they sound *just* like so-and-so! The artists recommended usually have a similar sound and/or style (i.e, hard rock, punk, etc.), but not exactly the same sound.

-Not all Christian artists will maintain the same style over time. Some groups may change their sound significantly from album to album. For example, D.C. Talk started out as a lightweight hip-hop group in the '80s, and became more alternative in the '90s. It's usually best to listen to the album first. Most Christian bookstores have demos you can listen to in the store. Ask a salesperson there for assistance.

-While we list many Christian artists here, we have not had the time to closely examine each and every new group that comes on the scene. Just as we would not recommend every church with the same enthusiasm, we cannot recommend every Christian artist with the same enthusiasm and confidence. It's important that you listen to Christian artists and discuss the music with your children, just as you would with mainstream artists.

4) We've tried to provide as many facts about each band as possible: significant albums, song lyrics, sales figures, quotes, newsworthy activities—whatever information we could find to enhance your understanding of each artist or group. We've tried to avoid rumor and speculation by documenting our profiles as much as possible. Our sources are cited in parentheses (with the date) following the fact or quote. Some resources (*e.g., SPIN, RIP,* and *People*) are spelled out in the profile. Others are abbreviated as shown below:

Abbreviation of Resources

AMG - *All Music Guide* (Michael Erlewine, ed., Miller Freeman Books, San Francisco, 1994)

AP - *Alternative Press*

APN - Associated Press News Service

BAM - *Bay Area Magazine*

BB - *Billboard*

BG - Boston Globe

CCM - *Contemporary Christian Music*

CDH - Chicago Daily Herald

CT - Chicago Tribune

DFP - Detroit Free Press

EW - *Entertainment Weekly*

FB - Fresno Bee

HM - *Heaven's Metal*

HP - *Hit Parader*

HRV - *Hard Rock Video*

IV - *Interview*

LAT - Los Angeles Times

MB - *Metal Blade*

MM - *Metal Maniacs*

NM - *New Music*

NME - *New Music Express*

NMR - *New Music Report*

NW - *Newsweek*

OPT - *Option*

PG - *Parental Guidance*

RB - *Rock Beat*

RC - Rock Confidential newsletter

RL - *Rock Lives* (by Timothy White, Holt & Co., New York, 1990)

RMS - *Rock Movers and Shakers* (Barry Lazell, ed., Billboard Publ., New York, 1989)

RS - *Rolling Stone*

RSE - *Rolling Stone's Encyclopedia of Rock and Roll* (Rolling Stone Press, New York, 1983)

SDR - San Diego Reader

SDU - San Diego Union/Tribune

SFC - San Francisco Chronicle

SH - *Star Hits*

SL - *Star Line*

STH - *Stairway To Heaven* (David Seay, with Mary Neely, Ballantine Books, New York, 1986)

TV - *TV Guide*

UER - *The Ultimate Encyclopedia of Rock* (Michael Heatley, ed., Harper-Collins, New York, 1993)

USA - USA Today

VF - *Vanity Fair*

Bible Versions:

KJV - King James Version

LB - Living Bible

NAS - New American Standard

NIV - New International Version

ROCK-N-ROLL PROFILES

FROM A(C/DC)
TO Z(Z TOP)

AC/DC

George Young's success in the mid-'60s with the Australian pop-rock band, the Easybeats, inspired his younger brothers to try *their* hand at rock-n-roll. When they started AC/DC in 1973, Malcolm (at 19) and Angus (at 14) were just a couple of skinny, pimply-faced lads who wanted to make loud rock music for other skinny, pimply-faced lads. They succeeded beyond their wildest dreams. They got their name from a tag on their sister's vacuum cleaner because they wanted a name that was loud and powerful, like their music. (For some time now, Christians have been claiming that AC/DC stands for "Anti-Christ/Devil's Children," but there is no documentation for this. In light of their beginnings, we always thought it meant "Acne Can/Devastate Children"!)

Since their early material was only being heard in Australia, they moved to England in 1976. *Let There Be Rock* (1977) made them famous there, and *Highway To Hell* (1979) broke them open in America. In the middle of all this success, singer Bon Scott died, drowning in his own vomit after a rowdy all-night drinking binge on February 19, 1980. He was replaced by Brian Johnson and the next album, *Back In Black* (1980), became their biggest hit, selling 13 million copies worldwide. *For Those About To Rock* (1981) became a #1 album in the U.S. and secured them the headlining spot at the Monsters of Rock Festival in England.

Their popularity peaked in 1983, but not their notoriety. They were thrust into the limelight in 1985 by the California serial killer Richard Ramirez, who was obsessed with the band and named himself The Night Stalker after one of their songs, "The Night Prowler." In 1991, the band drew attention again over three fans who were killed in the crush of the crowd at a concert in Salt Lake City. The band denied any responsibility for the tragedy.

Some still claim AC/DC encourages Satanism, mostly because of the devilish cover on *Highway To Hell*. There is some evidence that Bon Scott was exploring the occult, but those influences seemed to die with him. This band is known for their "naughty school boy" image, because of Angus' penchant for wearing knickers and mooning his audiences. Songs like "Big Balls," "You Shook Me All Night Long," and "Sink The Pink" clearly point to the fact that this band has always been more about sex than Satan. But just because they're not Satanists, doesn't mean Christians are free to get a charge out of AC/DC. After all, it's still true that "rebellion is as the sin of witchcraft, and stubbornness is as iniquity and idolatry" (1 Sam. 15:23, KJV).

Music Exchange: the Brave, Bride, Resurrection Band, Shout, X-Sinner, Whitecross

AEROSMITH
••

Formed in 1970, the band was originally a trio with Joe Perry on guitar, Tom Hamilton on bass, and Steven Tyler on drums. Tyler (who is the unofficial winner of the Mick Jagger lip look-alike contest) quit the band, but later rejoined as their singer. Their self-titled debut album (1973) featured "Dream On," which would become a Top Ten hit in 1976. *Toys In The Attic* (1975) sold over 6 million copies, and featured the initial version of "Walk This Way." By 1977, their popularity had pretty much peaked, and the band fell apart with excessive drinking and drugging, and a series of unremarkable solo projects.

They re-formed in 1984, without the drugs and alcohol (everyone in the band is either in Alcoholics Anonymous or Narcotics Anonymous), and walked this way into the glam metal movement. But they didn't completely reform. "Some people have a calling for Jesus, I have that in music," confesses Tyler. "Sex, drugs, and rock-n-roll! Take the drugs away, and there's more time for sex and rock-n-roll!" (*SPIN*, 1/88). Their career was revived with a new version of "Walk This Way" (1986), with rappers Run DMC. "Dude (Looks Like a Lady)" (1988) and "Love in an Elevator" (1989) kept them on top of the charts. In 1991, they signed a multi-album contract with Sony, reportedly worth $37 million. They were voted the best rock band in America in 1994—nearly a quarter of a century after they first began.

Basically, these are 40-year-old men still using rock to hustle 16-year-old girls. "I've always been sexually active," claims Tyler. "Why can't we do it all the time? We should be doing it three or four times a day. It's not being nasty. Everybody should be doing it!" (*RS*, 11/3/94). And sex they do. One reviewer described their album *Pump* (1989) as "big boy rock about doing it with big girls. Doing it in elevators, doing it hanging from clotheslines. These guys pare it down to what matters: sex, fun, fun sex, the blues, sex, the mall, and mascara everywhere" (*SPIN*, 11/89). Their only concession to "social consciousness" lies in an occasional song like "Janie's Got A Gun," about a woman who shoots the man who's abusing her—not exactly a healthy solution for what ails us.

Not everyone is happy with their sexual emphasis, of course. One young lady is quite offended by Tyler's approach to life. "He stands there and he's groping himself and he's 46 years old and should not be doing that!" Is this some prudish midwestern housewife? Guess again. It's model/actress Liv Tyler, Steven's 16-year-old daughter! (*TV*, 1/21/95). The younger generation always seems to rebel against the older one, doesn't it?

Music Exchange: Bride, Petra, Resurrection Band, Tamplin (Shout/Magdalen), White Heart, Whitecross, X-Sinner

ALICE IN CHAINS

This Seattle band actually hit the charts before fellow grunge-rockers **Nirvana** or **Pearl Jam**. Their debut album, *Facelift* (1991), contained the MTV video hit "Man in a Box," with its controversial

> "**W**hen someone asks me if I've found Jesus, I say, 'Yeah, I saw him at a Nirvana concert a couple of years ago!' "
> — *Tori Amos*

lyric "*Jesus Christ / deny your maker.*" The video included the image of a Christ figure with his eyes sewn shut, which seems to say God cannot see and does not care. After the albums *Dirt* (1992) and *Jar of Flies* (1994), the band began to fall apart—primarily because of singer Layne Staley's heroin habit, which kept the band from participating in either Woodstock II or the Lollapalooza Tour in 1994 (*EW*, 8/94).

"You can hardly tell from the oppressive darkness, gloom, and anguish of the songs on *Facelift*, but the band is composed of positive thinkers. They are positive that no matter how successful they become, they'll still have plenty of dark, gloomy, anguishing things to write about" (*LAT*, 9/1/91). Here's another group of grunge rockers selling nothing but depression to their fans, and too many of them are buying.

Music Exchange: Applehead, Clash of Symbols, Fell Venus, Grammatrain, Plankeye, Precious Death, Sometime Sunday, Yonderboy

Tori AMOS

The daughter of a Methodist minister, Amos has been playing piano since she was two, studying at the prestigious Peabody Conservatory at the tender age of five. She was kicked out at age 11 for rebelling against the rigid training, and she's been rebelling ever since. She's rejected her Christian upbringing for Celtic mythology and reincarnation, but she also rebels against feminist New Age women, who criticize her for being too sexual at her concerts. Amos' albums are a troubling mix of sexual and religious imagery. In the song "Icicle," she rejects communion in favor of masturbation: *"When they say 'take of this body' / I think I'll take from mine instead."* In the song "God," she chides: *"God, sometimes you just don't come through / Do you need a woman to look after you?"*

"When someone asks me if I've found Jesus, I say, 'Yeah, I saw him at a Nirvana concert a couple of years ago!' He's not going to fix things for me, I have to fix things for myself. We've just got to lighten up on the Savior bit, folks. You know, get off the cross. We need the wood!" (*SPIN*, 10/94).

Music Exchange: Jan Krist, Riki Michelle, Julie Miller, Leslie Phillips

ANTHRAX

You've got to admit it's a strange world when a band named after a sheep disease can become popular. This New York quintet originally formed in 1981, but their first popular album, *Among the Living*, wasn't released until 1987. The group was musically more diverse than most thrash bands. They dabbled in metal, punk, and rap, with a goofy, adolescent humor that gave them a reputation as The Three Stooges of Thrash. The group was put out to pasture in the early 1990s, overshadowed by the Seattle grunge scene.

For all their antics, Anthrax was just more of the same disguise. Underneath the silliness is the same cynicism too often found in today's music. They perpetuate a fascination with violence, death, and comic book sensationalism (they introduced their fans to underground comics like Judge Dredd and Teenage Mutant Ninja Turtles). The trap here is that kids may believe that humor covers a multitude of sins. The fans don't seem to care what these guys sing about, as long as it's fast, frantic, and funny. Everything else is simply swallowed with a grain of assault.

Music Exchange: Believer, MxPx, Precious Death

BAD RELIGION.

A couple of high school buddies started this band in 1980. It became the core of the early Los Angeles punk movement, along with the Germs, the Circle Jerks, Black Flag, Fear, and X. Although punk was supposedly dead by the mid-1980s, this band never really went away. They continued to pump out albums on their independently owned record label, Epitaph, which also produced **L7**'s early projects.

With the advent of the hardcore/punk revival in the '90s, this little label has become hugely popular, producing hit albums for bands like **Offspring** and **Rancid.** In the early 1990s, this band began to make its own comeback. A New Year's concert in 1990 broke out into a riot and gave the band the most press they'd seen in a decade. The album *Recipe for Hate* (1993) included a song called "American Jesus," which featured **Pearl Jam's** Eddie Vedder on vocals.

Unlike the mindless hedonism of metal, punk tends to be more intellectual with social/political themes. In Bad Religion's case, lead singer/writer Greg Graffin is in his early 30s and has a Master's degree in geology from UCLA (he's working on a Ph.D in vertebrate paleontology, i.e., dinosaurs). But just because he's smart doesn't mean he's wise. Graffin's music is full of liberal views on evolution, abortion, and anti-establishment sentiments. It's not so much that this band preaches directly against Christianity, although they have an intellectual disdain for what they perceive as its mindlessness. However, they are exactly what Paul had in mind when he said, "Don't let others spoil your faith and joy with their philosophies—their wrong and shallow answers built on men's ideas, instead of on what Jesus has said" (Col. 2:8, LB). Listening to this band may not give you a bad religion, but it might leave you with a bad taste for the One you have.

Music Exchange: Blenderhead, MxPx, early Undercover

The BEACH BOYS

Perhaps the biggest pre-Beatles pop group ever, the Beach Boys virtually invented the California surf rock sound in the '60s. Thirty years later, they are still one of the all-time biggest nostalgia favorites. Most of the band's favorite summer fun songs ("Surfin' U.S.A.," "Fun, Fun, Fun," "California Girls," "I Get Around," etc.) were produced between 1963 and 1965. Brian Wilson's *Pet Sounds* (1966) was the most innovative studio project produced up to that time, preceding the Beatles' *Sgt. Pepper's* by a full year. Running out of hits, the group moved to the nostalgia tour circuit by the mid-1970s. They had a brief resurgence in the '80s (helped somewhat by David Lee Roth's cover of "California Girls"), with their #1 hit "Kokomo" (1988), which is replayed endlessly on "Full House" reruns.

But for all the "good, clean fun" memories the band brings, the group's private lives were a rock-and-roller coaster ride. Brian Wilson's drug use led to a mental breakdown in 1965, and he remains virtually dysfunctional today. After a brief interlude with the Manson family, Dennis Wilson died in a drunken drowning accident in 1983. Cousin Mike Love met the Maharishi Mahesh Yogi in 1968, and continues to be devoted to TM and Eastern mysticism. Every member of the band has had marital problems. While little of this is reflected in their music, the Beach Boys have not been ideal role-models for the average Christian.

Music Exchange: the Swirling Eddies

The BEATLES

Most Americans never suspected that when the Fab Four invaded our living rooms back in 1964, John, Paul, George, and Ringo would change the face of rock-n-roll forever. The Beatles have their beginnings in 1957, when 17-year-old John Lennon invited 15-year-old Paul McCartney to play in his skiffle band, the Quarrymen. After adding George Harrison on guitar, Stu Sutcliffe on bass, and Peter Best on drums, they renamed themselves the Silver Beatles, emulating Buddy Holly's Crickets. They played clubs in Hamburg, Germany doing cover tunes of Buddy Holly, Chuck Berry, and Little Richard. McCartney took over on bass, when Sutcliffe decided to stay in Hamburg to paint (dying a year later of a brain hemorrhage). Best was dismissed in 1962, and was replaced by Ringo Starr.

When record store owner Brian Epstein began to manage them in 1962, they released the first hit single, "Love Me Do." What followed was a string of 12 #1 hits in Britain. Beatlemania was born. Americans didn't catch on until Ed Sullivan booked them for two Sundays in February, 1964. By April, the Beatles were holding all top five positions on the *Billboard* single charts at once ("Can't Buy Me Love," "Twist and Shout," "She Loves You," "I Want to Hold Your Hand," and "Please Please Me")— a feat that has never been duplicated. Eventually, there would be 20 #1 hit singles in America.

Their first film, *A Hard Day's Night*, was followed by record-setting concerts, the movie *Help!*, and the album *Rubber Soul* (1965). In 1966, they decided to quit touring, and retreated to their studio to produce their most experimental albums, *Revolver* and *Sgt. Pepper's Lonely Hearts Club Band* (1967). They joined Donovan (they call him Mellow Yellow) and Mike Love (of the **Beach Boys**) in India to follow the teachings of the Maharishi Mahesh Yogi. Lennon left after a few months, disgusted with the Yogi's hypocrisy, but George Harrison (who wrote "My Sweet Lord" for Krishna) continues to be a devotee. "Hey Jude" sold 6 million copies, becoming their biggest-selling single. *Yellow Submarine*, a full-length animated film based on their song, was followed by *The Beatles* double album, also known as the *White Album*.

Epstein's death in 1967 marked the beginning of the Beatles' breakdown. The *Magical Mystery Tour* film was panned as too self-indulgent, and the album yielded some of Lennon's most cryptic songs ever: "Strawberry Fields Forever" and "I Am the Walrus." Their record company, Apple Corps, signed James Taylor, Badfinger, and Mary Hopkin ("Those Were the Days"), but it became a financial disaster. But it was Lennon's association with Yoko Ono that broke any bonds the Beatles may have had left. *Abbey Road* marked the end of their "Long and Winding Road," and McCartney announced that the Beatles were officially over in April, 1970.

Lennon continued creating music, using it as primal therapy to express his rage over a father he never had and a mother who died too soon (when he was 18). Protesting the Vietnam war, he turned his honeymoon with Yoko Ono into a week-long "Bed-In" in 1969, and gave us the tune "Give Peace a Chance." He performed occasionally with Yoko as the Plastic Ono Band. He was murdered on December 8, 1980, soon after he got his first #1 hit in years, "Just Like Starting Over."

McCartney continued to write silly love songs and toured with his wife Linda Eastman in a band called Wings. He's had a number of successful solo singles, and several popular duets with the likes of **Michael Jackson** and Stevie Wonder. After some controversy over being caught with pot, McCartney has basically settled into the image of a stable family man.

George Harrison's spiritual beliefs continue to be reflected in his albums. He organized the Concert for Bangladesh in 1971. He joined Jeff Lynne (ELO), **Bob Dylan**, Tom Petty, and Roy Orbison to record as The Traveling Wilburys in 1988. (Orbison died of a heart attack only weeks after the album's release). Two years later, the remaining quartet record-ed a second album, inexplicably called *Vol. 3*, which went platinum like the first album. Harrison's own albums have only been marginally suc-cessful, but he remains active in environmental and political issues.

Ringo Starr had a couple of successful singles: "It Don't Come Easy" (1971), "Photograph" and "You're Sixteen" (1973). He's stayed visible act-ing in some strange films, including: *The Magic Christian* (1970), Frank Zappa's *200 Motels* (1971), and *Caveman* (1980). Starr's most well-known post-Beatles work is perhaps his role as the narrator for the children's TV special "Thomas the Tank Engine," which became a worldwide hit series "The Shining Time Station." In 1989, Ringo began touring with his All-Starr band. He was all over American TV in 1995 doing commercials for a credit card, and one for pizza that spoofed the on-going desire for a Beatles reunion (in the commercial he ends up with the Monkees instead).

Lennon's death pretty much killed any hopes for a reunion. Julian Lennon (John's son from his first marriage) had some hit singles which demonstrated a remarkable vocal likeness to his father, but no tour ever developed. There was talk that John and Yoko's son, Sean, might fit the bill, but again, nothing materialized. Finally, 25 years after the breakup, "The Beatles Anthology" was released in 1995. Featuring hours of film footage, the project is fueled by a new release called "Free As A Bird"—an unfinished Lennon tune actually sung by him and beefed up by the rest of the Beatles and today's technology. As Ringo observed, "It sounds like the bloody Beatles!" (*NW*, 10/23/95) It's the closest we'll get to a reunion in this lifetime.

"The impact of the Beatles—not only on rock-n-roll, but on all of Western culture—is simply incalculable" (*RSE,* pg. 32). "The Beatles were, quite simply, phenomenal: they changed lives, they changed pop music, they changed the world" (*UER*, pg. 180). But how did they change us? They gave us some interesting music and some innovative recording techniques. They also taught us to experiment with psychedelic drugs and introduced us to Marxism and eastern religions. It is not an exagger-ation to say that they fueled a revolution in rock which fueled a revolu-tion in attitude against the "military-industrial" complex, Viet Nam, the status quo, the establishment, and America as it had been defined for twenty years. But don't expect your kids to get it. They never knew a pre-Beatles America, and can't comprehend how profoundly the Beatles affected their generation.

The Beatles have been analyzed in dozens of books. There's only one thing I'd like to add here. John Lennon's rebellion is clearly connected to his lack of a stable family life. He says so himself in the song "Mother." His anguish foreshadows all the rebellious grunge rockers and punk slackers to come. It also explains his anger at God and the church. His infamous comments about being bigger than Jesus were considered blasphemous, but most people missed the disappointment under the proclamation. Here's the complete quote, delivered soon after he'd read *The Passover Plot,* a then-popular attempt to debunk the resurrection of Christ: "Christianity will go. It will vanish and shrink. I needn't argue about that. I'm right and will be proved right. Jesus was alright, but his disciples were thick and ordinary. It's them twisting it that ruins it for me. We [the Beatles] are more popular than Jesus Christ right now" (*RL,* pg. 117-118).

He was wrong, of course, about the demise of Christianity. Lennon and Nietzsche may be dead, but God isn't. However, he was right on one point. The Beatles at the time were more popular than Jesus Christ. Pop culture will always be *popular.* The sacrificial life of Christ never will be. Angry young men still continue to challenge the authority of God and church and parents. But like Lennon, many of these young men don't have a clear picture of what it is they're defying. It's hard to believe in a strong, stable, loving Father if your father was never around. It's hard to imagine a healthy, happy heaven if your home life is an angry war zone. Either extreme of absence or abuse in the home will inevitably produce a rebellious child. But their rebellion doesn't absolve the rest of us from presenting a clear, untwisted portrait of the character of Christ.

Music Exchange: Brighton, Phil Keaggy (esp. *Sunday's Child* album), the Kry, One Hundred Days, Pray For Rain, Randy Stonehill, Villanelle

BECK.
• •

This rap/folk/blues rocker from Chicago fashioned a music career from his slacker attitude and today's blink-and-you-miss-it, throw-away pop culture. "Beck creates music that celebrates the junk culture of the '70s and '80s, but Beck is distinctly a product of the '90s: all of his influences come through television and records, not from real life experiences. That trashy, disposable quality is what makes his music special" (*AMG,* pg. 34). "He's just a kid who wrote a song that makes no sense at all," said a fan in Houston. "Then he makes a video that looks like it was done in his backyard, and he probably didn't even think it would get on MTV, but it did, and now he's making a bunch of money. It's really pretty funny" (*E.W.,* 4/8/94). So much for the myth of the sophisticated music industry.

Beck is a prime example of the Absurdist philosophy in rock today (see "The Four Philosophies of Rock," pg. XXX). His hit single was an empty little ditty called "Loser" ("*I'm a loser, baby / So why don't you kill me*")—a lame attempt to rationalize the aimlessness of the latch-key generation (when all else fails, simply call your vices virtues). He parleyed the hit into an album contract and released *Mellow Gold* (a street reference to pot) in 1994. The album is musically diverse, drawing on hip-hop, folk, psychedelic pop, and rock styles. The lyrics are sarcastic satires saying that life is as cheap and valueless as the throw-away pop culture we live in today. But it isn't the culture that's crippling us. It's this constant focus on what losers we all are. Beck's fans would be better off if they just threw way this bit of pop trash and focused on finding some real meaning for their lives (Col. 3:2).

Music Exchange: Danielson, Imagine This

BELLY.
....

Singer/songwriter Tanya Donelly co-founded the Throwing Muses with her step-sister, Kristin Hersh, when the girls were only 15. Having stretched her writing abilities in bands like the **Breeders** and This Mortal Coil, Donelly left the Muses and formed Belly with several friends from her hometown in Newport, Rhode Island. Their first album, *Star* (1993), hit #1 on the college radio charts and sold better than all six Muses' albums combined. Her second album, *King* (1995), is filled with "songs of lust, love and betrayal" (*EW,* 2/17/95).

Belly offers a moodiness that is sometimes enchanting and sometimes eerie. "Her lyrics—poetic, twisted, and filled with an almost mystical sexuality—hint at a darker side to this girl next door" (*EW,* 2/17/95). Donelly draws many of her songwriting ideas from mythology and faery tales, as well as the news. "I get a lot of ideas from stories where I read about harmful, painful things that people do to each other. But it's mostly other people's pain" (*Option*, 9-10/93).

This kind of focus takes its toll, especially without a spiritual balance. It's not that Christians shouldn't be sensitive to the pain of others, but focusing on the world's worst, instead of God's best, leaves us with a lopsided view of life. "I'm a very spiritual person," claims Donelly, "but I haven't found God yet" (*EW,* 4/16/93). We hope Tanya finds what she's looking for some day soon.

Music Exchange: Dakota Motor Company, Julie Miller, Morella's Forrest, Nina, Leslie Phillips (esp., *The Turning*), Sixpence None The Richer

Jello BIAFRA. See The DEAD KENNEDYS.

Björk.

This little pop-pixie from Iceland, arrived on American shores in the late '80s with her band, the Sugarcubes. The off-kilter punk-pop of their debut album *Life's Too Good* (1988) earned them the critical hype of "coolest band in the world." The albums that followed were considered disappointments, and Björk (who's now 30) left Iceland and the band to live in London and raise her son (the product of a brief marriage to a Sugarcube named Thor). Her first solo effort, *Debut* (1993), sold 2.5 million copies. Her latest album, *Post* (1995), is an eccentric effort that swings between techno post-punk like "Army of Me" and a 1940s era big band spoof called "Blow A Fuse (It's So Quiet)."

Björk has been described as quirky, eccentric, a magic faery, and just plain weird. From her unique way of phrasing a song to her Heidi-goes-haywire hairdo's, there is little that is middle-of-the-road or mainstream about her. She's been accused of occultism (paganism is an official religion in Iceland, and she has a circle of mysterious runes tattooed on her arm—she calls it her compass), but it doesn't show up in her music. She talks in a mile-a-minute free-association that makes her sound like she's on drugs. (While she seems to go to clubs and get drunk on a regular basis, there's little evidence for other types of drug use).

Having grown up in a permissive hippie environment, where she was allowed to do whatever she wanted, she became a free thinker. Perhaps too free. Chronically impulsive, she approaches life with a no-thought-is-unthinkable, no-behavior-is-too-bizarre attitude. Some call this freedom, others call it chaos. The bible teaches that God set certain limits to help us find order and purpose in our lives. Those who live beyond those borders, may not always be consciously trying to defy God, but they ultimately will embrace their own self-destruction.

Music Exchange: Riki Michelle, Julie Miller, Out of the Grey

BLACK CROWES

This blues-rock band from Atlanta has been called America's young Rolling Stones (accent on the "stoned"). Their first album, *Shake Your Moneymaker* (1990), offered some of the grittiest songs about getting drunk and being lonely since Janis Joplin. The album *Amorica* (1994) was banned in many stores because of the album cover—a revealing photo of a woman's (far too) tiny bikini bottom.

Drugs and alcohol feature prominently in their real lives, as well as their songs. On their first major tour in 1991, singer Chris Robinson was arrested because he refused to accept a clerk's explanation that it's illegal to sell alcohol after midnight in Colorado. After going into an angry tirade and spitting on her, he walked off with two cases of beer which he refused to pay for. The group also puts a lot of effort into the Atlanta Pot Festival each year to help legalize marijuana.

The band was kicked off a summer tour with **ZZ Top** for their constant mockery of the beer company that sponsored them. It seems their standards are too high to accept support from the corrupt corporation selling beer, but not from the corrupt corporation selling their records. This is one of those cocky young bands that talks like they've got all the answers, but they're just blowing smoke. (Prov. 10:14; cf., Prov. 12:16; 12:23; 14:16; 18:2, 6-7; 19:3; 20:3).

Music Exchange: Greg Chaisson, Guardian, Chris Lizotte, Third Day

BLACK FLAG. See Henry Rollins.

BLACK SABBATH

Formed in 1968 in Birmingham, England, they were originally called Earth. They had their first radio hit in 1971 with a song called "Paranoid" from an album originally called *War Pigs*. Constant touring helped them become more popular in the U.S. (and in Europe) than back home in England. "Despised by rock critics and ignored by radio, Sabbath still managed to sell over 7 million albums" (*RSE*, pg. 46). Singer **Ozzy Osbourne** left the band for a successful solo career in 1979. Guitarist Tony Iommi continues to tour and record as Black Sabbath, but despite famous replacements like Ronnie James Dio, Sabbath has never managed to recapture its mid-70s popularity.

Black Sabbath explored the occult as a curiosity and used the imagery to sell more albums. There is little evidence that they practiced Satanism as a lifestyle or that they ever truly adopted it as a personal belief system. But they kept everyone guessing as much as possible with their interviews and public image. "We're into God," said Iommi once. "But sometimes," added Ozzy maliciously, "I think Satan *is* God" (*Metallion*, 6/86). Eventually, they dropped the imagery altogether—except for 1989's *Headless Cross* album, when Iommi tried to sell the old image to a new breed of death metal fans. The album went virtually unnoticed.

But just because they're not *real* Satanists doesn't make them suddenly okay to listen to. "Black Sabbath dealt in songs of death, destruction, demonic possession, evil occurrences and all manner of loathsome horrors from the dark side of the mind" (*Metallion*, 6/86). It's just that no one listens to this band much any more, except as a historical curiosity. And the newer bands espousing Satanism, like **King Diamond** and **Deicide**, are far more serious and sinister than Sabbath ever dreamed of being. Like the devil himself, Christians have given Black Sabbath too much credence and attention.

Music Exchange: Rose, Sardonyx

Mary J. BLIGE

This New York native began singing gospel in her mother's church at the tender age of 7, and produced her first album at the age of 21. Her debut album, *What's the 411?* (1992), went platinum. Her second album, *My Life* (1994), broadened her popularity beyond the soul and hip-hop circles. Blige mixes a soulful R&B singing style with a hip-hop image that has earned her the label of the Ghetto Princess. She is one of the few women doing this style (called New Jack Swing—sometimes called New Jill Swing, when a woman does it), usually the domain of male-dominated groups like Silk, Shai, Guy or **Jodeci.**

While the music is a nice mix, her message seems to be a bit mixed up. While filming a music video for the tune "You Bring Me Joy," Blige relaxes between takes with "the chronic and some 40's" (marijuana and 40 oz. bottles of malt liquor) (*IV*, 7/95). Raised in the church, "she speaks of God in the personal way one might refer to their mother or father" (*SOURCE*, 1/95). But she sings about sex just as intimately: *"Come into my bedroom, honey / What I got will make you spend money."* While her songs are described as sensitive, she seems to have become chronically *in*sensitive to the conflict between her flesh and her spirit.

Music Exchange: Angie & Debbie (Winans), Out of Eden

BLIND MELON.
· ·
Formed in L.A. in 1990, this band's Southern-fried, psychedelic folk-rock brought them comparisons to the **Grateful Dead**. Their self-titled debut (1992) eventually sold 2 million copies due to MTV's incessant airing of the video for "No Rain," the one with the plump little "Bee Girl" doing her awkward ballet. It also got them a slot at the Woodstock II festival during the summer of 1994. Their second album, *Soup*, wasn't released until 1995. The delay was partly due to singer Shannon Hoon's arrest for drunk and disorderly conduct while recording the album in New Orleans, and generally just "sobering everybody up and getting them there" (*CDH*, 7/10/95).

Hoon was also arrested for getting naked at a concert in Vancouver and urinating on his audience. His reason? "A concert should be a time for a band and their fans to do whatever they want" (*AP*, 11/3/93). Later he was arrested at the American Music Awards for starting a brawl during the taping (*AP*, 2/24/94). "The guy was definitely excessive in everything," confesses guitarist Rogers Stevens. "He was excessive in his violent tendencies and excessive in all areas of his life" (*RS*, 11/30/95).

Despite their '60s sound, there's no peace-and-love hippie vibe here. Hoon was vocal about his disgust for Christianity and his admiration of Nietzsche, who said "God is dead" (*RIP*, 11/93). God's not dead, but Nietzsche is. And now, so is Hoon. Despite several trips to drug rehabilitation centers, he died of a drug overdose (heroin?) on October 21, 1995 at the age of 28. He apparently died on the tour bus in New Orleans, just as the band was launching an 18-month concert tour to promote *Soup* (*EW*, 11/3/95). This band's anger and excess offer nothing for the Christian listener. Don't be blind — use your melon and listen to Christian music instead.

Music Exchange: Greg Chaisson, Resurrection Band

Michael BOLTON
••

Bolton's bombastic and impassioned vocals have earned him a strong following, especially among hopelessly romantic females. He is better known for his covers than for his original music. He sailed to the top of the charts with songs like "Sittin' On the Dock of the Bay," "When A Man Loves a Woman," and "How Am I Supposed To Live Without You?" Bolton is often castigated by rock critics for his overblown, blue-eyed soul as "someone who sings the blues without paying the dues." But his music is basically of a harmlessly romantic nature—except for those young ladies who have become more pre-occupied with falling in love with love than following the Lord of love.

Music Exchange: Bob Carlisle, Clay Crosse, Bryan Duncan, John Elephante (of Mastedon), Matthew Ward

BOYZ II MEN
••

These four teens walked out of Philadelphia's School of Creative and Performing Arts right into the music business. An informal audition with Michael Bivins (of Bell Biv Devoe) led them to a Motown record contract. Their first album, *Cooleyhighharmony* (1991), sold over 7 million copies with its smooth harmonies on ballads like "It's So Hard To Say Goodbye to Yesterday." It earned the group an American Music Award for Favorite New Soul Artist, a Grammy for Best New Artist, and a slew of imitators like All4One, Silk, and Shai.

For the most part, this group avoids the violent images of most rappers and the sexual badgering of R&B groups like Shai, Guy, or **Jodeci**. They are proud of their clean-cut, positive image, and they try to practice old-fashioned, traditional values. When asked if they are religious, they respond: "Very. God is a huge part of our lives—every day, in everything we do. We wouldn't be where we are without Him" (*LAT*, 10/3/93). "I Want To Make Love To You" is a mildly troubling tune, and it remains to be seen if this is simply a rare attempt at seduction or a more prominent part of their message as they grow older. The other problem with the group is that you have to endure sexually-explicit opening acts like **Montell Jordan** or **TLC** when you see them in concert.

Music Exchange: Church of Rhythm, Dawkins & Dawkins, LaMore, Take 6

Toni BRAXTON

Like many soul singers (e.g., Anita Baker or Whitney Houston, to whom she is often compared), Braxton learned to sing in the church. Her father's an Apostolic minister who forbade her to listen to the kind of music she now sings. Braxton came to public attention with the ballad "Love Should Have Brought You Home" from the Eddie Murphy film *Boomerang* (1993).

Most of Braxton's songs are about lost love, and there is nothing overtly evil in her music. If there is a caution here, it lies in Braxton's tendency to secularize Christian ideas—heaven is something you find in a lover's arms, and angels are beautiful women to fall in love with. Braxton explains her song "Speaking in Tongues" as a ballad about "the sounds people make when they make love" (*EW*, Fall/1993). It is important to put the Gospel in terms today's world can understand. But we should be cautious when singers reverse the process and couch spiritual realities in terms of sexual innuendo.

Music Exchange: Angie & Debbie (Winans), Nicole, CeCe Winans

The BREEDERS

This three-woman, one-man band is another quirky, post-punk, college radio favorite. Kim Deal started the group as a side-project while she was still with The Pixies. The first two albums featured Tanya Donelly of the Throwing Muses and **Belly**. The project now features Kim's twin sister, Kelly, who did not know how to play the guitar when she was asked to join the band as their guitarist! Kelly, 33, was later arrested and indicted as a drug dealer when she signed for a package that contained 4 grams of heroin. Although she claims she didn't know what was in the package, she asked for treatment in a drug rehab center to avoid jail time (*APN*, 5/22/95).

Like many modern rock outfits, the music creates strong moods, while the lyrics are difficult to decipher. The Breeders' jangly guitar work projects an upbeat spirit that's downright infectious. However, the girl's goofy-sister persona covers some sex-obsessed lyrics. Kim describes "No Aloha" as about the "big slut scene" and the song "Divine Hammer" as "just like a big orgasm" (*OPT,* 5-6/93). "Isn't that what all the songs are about?" asks the bassist (*RS*, 10/28/93). For all its infectious fun, Christians need to be careful about what this kind of music may infect them with.

Music Exchange: Dakota Motor Company, Hoi Polloi, Julie Miller, Morella's Forest, Nina, Leslie Phillips, Sixpence None the Richer

Garth BROOKS
....

Garth Brooks is undoubtedly the biggest selling country artist of all time. He once had four albums in the Top Twenty at the same time and is the only artist to have two albums sell over 10 million copies each—a feat not even **Michael Jackson** has duplicated. One reason for his broad popularity is his use of rock-n-roll techniques during his concerts, including flash explosions and flying out over his audience on a wire harness. (Brooks confesses that **KISS** was one of his biggest influences growing up.)

Brooks also gained attention for moving beyond the "crying in my beer" lyrics of traditional country music to '90s-style themes of social controversy. His song "The Thunder Rolls" was an unflinching look at domestic violence, but the graphic violence and lingering look at adultery in the video kept it off Country Music Television (*Billboard*, 5/11/91). Like Aerosmith's "Janie's Got A Gun," the video seems to advocate that murder by a battered woman is justified.

Brooks joined P-FLAG (Parents and Friends of Lesbians and Gays) when his bass-playing sister revealed that she was gay. Brooks received an award from GLAAD (the Gay and Lesbian Alliance Against Defamation) for his song "We Shall Be Free." The award is given for the song that best depicts freedom of sexual choice. The song called for the freedom *"to love anyone we choose"* (*USA*, 1/27/93). Although he is often heralded as a "family values' kind of guy, Christians need to ask themselves what kind of family Brooks envisions.

Music Exchange: Brian Barrett, Steven Curtis Chapman, Ken Holloway, Michael James, MidSouth, Paul Overstreet

BUSH
....

This grunge rock quartet sounds like they were raised in Seattle, rather than in their native London. Their music is far closer to **Pearl Jam** or **Nirvana,** than the pop-synth sounds that usually come out of England these days. The band's name has a double-meaning. Singer Gavin Rossdale alludes to it as a reference to genital anatomy (*RS*, 7/13-27/94). But it's also a British term for pot (marijuana), which Rossdale admits is his favorite vice (*SPIN*, 6/95). The album *Sixteen Stone* (1994) is full of angst-ridden vocals, distorted guitars, and cryptic lyrics about sex, violence, and Elvis. The first radio/MTV hit was "Everything Zen," a distorted statement about disillusionment. The rest of the album reflects a cynical slacker attitude along the lines of **Green Day**, with songs like "Testosterone," which mocks machismo and lyrics like, "*We're so bored / You're to blame.*" It's high time kids started realizing that buying into these attitudes is a wasted time.

Music Exchange: Curious Fools, Hocus Pick, Precious Death, Raspberry Jam, Sometime Sunday, Yonderboy

CANNIBAL CORPSE.

This gory band may be the best (or worst) example of the "over-the-top" death and dismemberment mentality known as death metal. Their stage shows follow Alice Cooper's school of Shock Rock, and they got some unnecessary national attention as the band in the movie *Ace Ventura: Pet Detective*. Their music has been described as "...sickly, brutal metal, spewed at a nauseating pace by five psychotic sickos...it will satisfy the needs of the sickest death metal fans" (*MB*, 9/91). Subtle clues as to their philosophy can be found in album titles such as *Eaten Back to Life* (1990), *Butchered At Birth* (1991), *Mutilated* (1993), and *The Bleeding* (1994). And there are songs like "Rancid Amputation," "Innards Decay" ("*Rotting alive / Tearing my way through the meat / Driven to kill / My brain twitching for guts*"), or the tender love song "Meathook Sodomy". "We're on a mission to expose the most grotesque," says the band's singer/songwriter, Chris Barnes. "We want people to look at some blood. Violence and gore are still entertaining" (*RIP*, 9/91). Looking at blood is cool! Unless we're talking about the blood of Christ, of course.

Music Exchange: Crimson Thorn, Living Sacrifice, Mortification

Mariah CAREY.

Rock fans may mock her and some industry-types are cynical about her rise to fame because of her marriage to Tommy Mattola, head of Columbia Records and Sony Music—but her albums sales speak volumes about her true popularity.

Taught to sing by a mother who is a vocal coach for the New York City Opera Company, Maria Carey has simpy become one of the most popular artists of all time. So far, since the release of her self-titled debut album in 1990, she's sold over 60 million albums worldwide—more than all the albums sold by **Nirvana** and **Pearl Jam** combined! Her third album, *Music Box* (1994), has sold over 24 million alone. She is the only artist in the history of the Billboard Hot 100 charts to have every one of her first nine singles make it to the Top Five; she's the first female singer to a have a song debut at #1 on the singles charts; she's had nine #1 singles already in her relatively brief career (*EW,* 10/6/95).

Mariah's romantic R&B is obviously influenced by gospel music styles. Although, she's not a professing Christian, she cites gospel artists like the Clark Sisters and Shirley Caesar as her favorite music. Like some of her romantic counterparts (e.g., **Toni Braxton**, Whitney Houston), she tends to spiritualize romantic love by shrouding it in church terminology (i.e., being in love is invariably like being in heaven, etc.) On her album, *Daydream* (1995), she seems to be trying to broaden her street credibility with hip-hop tunes like "Fantasy," a duet with hardcore rapper Ol' Dirty Bastard.

However, her love songs are relatively pure, positive, and devoid of the sexual come-ons found in most dance music today. Songs like "Make It Happen" from *Emotions* (1991) could compete with any tune on the contemporary gospel charts today. Frankly, she's refreshingly rare in secular music, and hopefully she'll "Carey" on!

Music Exchange: Gina, Lavine Hudson, Crystal Lewis, Nicole

CARNIVORE. See TYPE-O-NEGATIVE.

Mary CHAPIN-CARPENTER
••

Mary Chapin-Carpenter is not a conventional country artist. Raised in Princeton, New Jersey, her father is a publisher at *Life* magazine. She graduated from Brown University with a degree in American Civilization. Her music is closer to folk-rock and rockabilly than pure country, but she's been voted Best Female Artist by the Academy of Country Music in 1989 and received a Grammy for Best Female Country Performance in 1992.

Most of her songs are about the dawning feminism among Southern women who are no longer entranced by Billy-Bob's macho moves. She rejects TV Christianity in "I Take My Chances": "*I found a preacher who spoke of the Light, but there was brimstone in his throat / He'd show me The Way, according to him / In exchange for my personal check / I flipped the channel back to CNN, and lit another cigarette.*" That's the trouble with trying to find religion through the media. We tend to pay more attention to the messenger than the message and miss the Author altogether.

Music Exchange: Susan Ashton, Margaret Becker, Kim Hill, Carol Huston, Andi Landis, Serene & Pearl

Eric CLAPTON

Eric "Slowhand" CLAPTON is one of rock's original guitar heroes. He joined the Yardbirds in 1963, a band which would later feature guitar wizards Jeff Beck and Jimmy Page (later with **Led Zeppelin**). During this time, graffiti began to appear all over London saying "Clapton is God." He formed Cream in 1966, which had hits in 1968 with "White Room" and "Sunshine of Your Love." He also recorded "While My Guitar Gently Weeps" with George Harrison of **the Beatles.**

Clapton formed Blind Faith in 1969 with Steve Winwood (of Traffic). During this time, Clapton reportedly accepted Christ, a faith he has denied and reaffirmed several times during his career. This was when Clapton wrote "Presence of the Lord" (which Christian artist Glenn Kaiser later covered on REZ's *Silence Screams* album in 1988). Next came a tour with Delaney and Bonnie, out of which he formed Derek & the Dominos. The hit song "Layla" (1970) was a tribute to George Harrison's wife Patti, whom Clapton later married (1979) and divorced (1986). His hit "After Midnight" later became a hit beer commercial. By the early 1970s, Clapton's heroin addiction began to slow Slowhand down.

> **"This is definitely not hopeful music, you know. I'm not offering them hope. I'm not offering them anything, really."**
> **- Adam Duritz of Counting Crows**

When he beat his habit, he came back with hits like Bob Marley's "I Shot the Sheriff" (1974), "Knockin' on Heaven's Door" (1975), and "Lay Down Sally" (1978). In the 1980s, he played on **Phil Collin's** early solo efforts and wrote scores for movies like *Lethal Weapon*. The 1990s brought much tragedy to Clapton. In 1990, he lost three members of his band in a helicopter accident, which also claimed the life of blues guitarist Stevie Ray Vaughn. In 1991, his four-year-old son fell out of the window of their 53rd story apartment. Clapton's tribute to him, "Tears in Heaven," was heartfelt and earned him six belated Grammies in 1993.

Clapton's life defines the legacy of rock-n-roll. Musically talented and personally unstable, Clapton has seen the heights of being called God and the depths of facing his demons in heroin and alcohol. He has seen personal fame and riches and personal tragedy. It is unclear where he stands with the Lord today, but it is perfectly clear why he plays the blues.

Music Exchange: Rex Carroll, Greg Chaisson, Glenn Kaiser, Phil Keaggy, Dana Key, Chris Lizotte

COLLECTIVE SOUL

This five-peice pop-rock band from Atlanta, Georgia almost never came together. Singer/songwriter Ed Roland had been looking for a way into the music world for a decade and had decided to give up on being in a band. When a demo of songs he hoped to publish found its way on to some college radio, he had to reform his band to get signed by Atlantic Records.

Their debut album, *Hints, Allegations, and Things Left Unsaid* (1994), produced the hit "Shine," a catchy gospel-pop plea for inspiration. It opened the door for an appearance at Woodstock II that summer, and an opening slot on the **Aerosmith** tour that fall. Their second album, *Collective Soul* (1995), is a little darker musically, but the positive spirituality is still there. For example, "Simple," the first hit off the album, is a churning ode to the power of love.

This group presents a bit of a paradox. Roland is open about being brought up in the church and the fact that his dad is a Southern Baptist minister—and doesn't seem the slightest bit bitter or angry about it. However, he is not as forthcoming about the state of his own Christianity, and the band's name is derived from a concept in Ayn Rand's humanist novel *Fountainhead*. His lyrics are steeped in the language of the church, and his basic philosophy does seem fairly healthy. There is a positive hopefulness in the lyrics ("Shine," "Love Lifted Me") and an unswerving faith in the power of love ("Simple," "Collection of Goods").

There are some dark doubts, mostly reflected by others in his songs ("The World I Know," "When The Water Falls"), but he is asking the right questions, not railing against the unseen hand of God. He looks at the betrayal and dark lives of others ("December," "Wasting Time," "Where the River Flows") without letting it change his own path.

There's a confidence and self-assurance in these lyrics that is rarely reflected in the angry angst of most alternative music (an attitude he critiques in "Smashing Young Man"). So while this is not a "Christian" band, per se, they are almost as positive in their message as any Christian rock band today.

Music Exchange: Daniel Amos, the Dell Griffiths, Johnny Q. Public, poor old lu

COLOR ME BADD

This quartet performs a unique blend of smooth doo-wop and rough-edged hip hop. They are most notable for their first hit single, "I Wanna Sex You Up" (on the soundtrack of the violent, urban film, *New Jack City*) in 1990. Neither their themes nor their popularity have been quite as notable since then. Talented though they may be, since their popularity rests on such a blatant sexual come-on, they don't come on our recommended list.

Music Exchange: Audio Adrenaline, Church of Rhythm, DC Talk, Rhythm & News

COOLIO

This is another in a seemingly endless stream of gansta rappers, distinguished mostly by his distinctive dreadlocked hairstyle. Like **NWA** and **Dr. Dre,** he is from the city of Compton (in Los Angeles). His top-selling album is full of violence ("County Line"), explicit sex ("Hand on My Nutsack," "Ugly Bitches"), smoking dope ("Smokin' Stix") and making it seem cool to steal ("It Takes a Thief"). His hit single "Fantastic Voyage" summarizes his dead-end approach to life: "*I do what I do to survive / That's why I pack my .45 / Life is a bitch and then you die.*" How original. And wrong.

Music Exchange: Dynamic Twins, Grits, S.F.C., S.S. M.O.B., T-Bone

ALICE COOPER

Alice was born Vincent Furnier, the son of a minister. Legend has it that he was contacted by a distant dead relative at a seance—a 17th century witch who'd been burned at the stake. The witch promised him fame and fortune if she could reside in his body, and he agreed and became Alice Cooper. Starting out as "the worst bar band in Los Angeles," he became the forerunner to every theatrical make-up band in history from **KISS** to Twisted Sister and from **Ozzy Osbourne** to **Nine Inch Nails**.

His peculiar brand of horror rock theatrics (which he called Shock Rock) peaked in popularity in 1975 with his Welcome to My Nightmare tour. There followed a number of years appearing on "Hollywood Squares" and at celebrity golf tournaments—and fighting a vicious bout with alcoholism. But like the undead he sang about, Alice just kept coming back. In 1983, Cooper got (and stayed) sober and came back with some stage shows he called "Splatter Rock."

In the early 1990s he came back again, this time reportedly "born again." His album *The Last Temptation* (1994) depicts a young man struggling with moral temptations who takes the high road to choose heaven rather than hell. All indications are that he is attending a church in Phoenix regularly and submitting future song material to his pastors for approval. Let's hope Alice really has offered his Last Temptation to today's youth.

Music Exchange: Liason, Novella, Siloam, the Stand, Ken Tamplin

COUNTING CROWS

This San Francisco-area rock band sold 4 million copies of their debut album, *August And Everything After* and was voted best new band of 1994 by *Rolling Stone* magazine. Their music is compared to everyone from **Van Morrison** to **Soul Asylum**. And like most '90s alternative rock bands, they are generally more intelligent than the mindless metal of the '80s. But their lyrics are decidedly dark and disillusioned. "The only reason I'm famous now," says Adam Duritz, the band's singer/songwriter, "is because of unhappiness. My misery is everybody else's entertainment" (*RS*, 6/30/94).

He admits that drinking and drugs contribute to his state of despair. And he's honest enough to admit that he has nothing to offer to the hopeless nihilism of this generation: "This is definitely not hopeful music, you know. I'm not offering them hope. I'm not offering them anything, really. If you think about it, the whole thing is pretty self-centered and bizarre" (*RS*, 6/30/94).

The CRANBERRIES

The CRANBERRIES are one of those Irish pop groups that are so popular with the college radio crowd today. Their sound is melodic and ethereal, reminiscent of the Cocteau Twins. Their first album, *Everybody Else Is Doing It, So Why Can't We?* (1993), sold over 2 million copies. Their second album, *No Need To Argue* (1994), offers dark observations of life and some compassion for those who suffer the ravages of war or broken relationships. The song "Zombie" bemoans the children who have been victimized in the Irish conflict. Songs like "The Icicle Melts," "Empty," and "Daffodil Lament" continue in the same bittersweet vein. Their music has been described as "dream-pop" (*RS*, 4/21/94), but their dreams never quite wake up to the reality of real love.

Music Exchange: Dakota Motor Company, Eden Burning, Fleming & John, Hoi Polloi, Iona, Raspberry Jam, Sixpence None the Richer

CRASH TEST DUMMIES

This Canadian group has found a niche with the modern rock college crowd. Their Celtic-tinged pop and artsy, tongue-in-cheek ideas appeal to intellectual alternative fans, if only for the challenge of interpreting the lyrics. Singer/songwriter Brad Roberts has degrees in literature and philosophy and had every intention of getting his Ph.D. and becoming a professor.

Their surprising musical success has temporarily sidelined those lofty aspirations. Their hummable hit "Mmm mmm mmmm" is typical of their smug humor as it pokes fun at life's losers. Their absurdist mindset is more amusing (and less mean-spirited) than most punk/alternative artists. But just because they're not bitter doesn't mean they're (spiritually) better.

Music Exchange: Eden Burning, Chris Lizotte, Rich Mullins

Sheryl CROW

Sheryl Crow was a music teacher from Missouri who left to find her fortune in Los Angeles after breaking up with her Christian fiancé who tried to persuade her to sing exclusively for the Lord (*People*, 9/12/94). Six months after her arrival, she landed a spot as a back-up singer for **Michael Jackson** on his world tour in 1987. She later wrote songs for **Eric Clapton** and Wynnona Judd and sang back-up for Don Henley of the Eagles.

Crow's music is a likeable, bluesy folk sound. Her songs are mostly stories about the troubled people she sees around her—people who struggle with drugs, money, and relationships. Crow had her own problems for awhile, falling into a severe depression that had her bed-ridden for six months. Therapy and anti-depressants allowed her to go on and share her bleak vision of life with us. Her vision may be honest, but it has honestly left God behind.

Music Exchange: Carolyn Arends, Susan Ashton, Ashley Cleveland, Ashton/Becker/Denton, Out of the Grey

The CURE

This British band was formed in 1976 during the gloom-punk trend known as Death Rock. They are part of a trio of groups (including **Depeche Mode** and Morrissey of the Smiths) that taught kids how to be happy about being hopeless. Their dark dance music appeared on a series of depressing albums.

Pornography (1982) has been called the definitive gothic album. *Head on the Door* (1985) is a series of nightmarish images that singer/songwriter Robert Smith experienced during heavy bouts of drinking. *Disintegration* (1989) was considered a happier album: "On this album, Smith comes across as merely terminally depressed, a mood that, for him, is positively giddy!" (*People*, 6/12/89). In between albums, Smith plays for goth-rock queen, Siouxsie and the Banshees. The Cure has reportedly "retired" several times, but they still occasionally put out bleak albums like *Wish* (1992).

Fans insist this is a fun band. After all, they're known to go to parties dressed as kitchen appliances (*SH*, 10/85)! But the band was best described in a concert review that declared "The Cure Builds a Mood of Quiet Despair" (*LAT*, 7/14/84). During a fierce hangover, Smith had the phrase "I am filled with an overwhelming desire to die!" written on his arm (*SH*, 10/85). He had a recurring dream that he would die on Valentine's Day, and when it didn't happen, he got *really* depressed.

Distraught over being jilted by a girlfriend, a fan got up on stage during the Cure's 1986 U.S. tour and stabbed himself repeatedly. The crowd of 18,000 cheered and urged him on, believing it to be part of the stage show (*RMS,* pg. 125).

A young lady at one of my seminars once told me that before she became a Christian, one of her favorite things to do when she came home from school, was to put her favorite Cure albums on the stereo and stare at the wall. The Cure has helped many girls like her to embrace emptiness and romanticize suicide. If they suffer from low self-esteem and focus on their pain long enough, they often end up in treatment centers for depression. This focus on death and depression has fueled the nihilism found in today's gothic and industrial music. This band truly is the cure for nothing.

Music Exchange: Code of Ethics, Dead Artist Syndrome, L.S.U., Luxury, Scarlet, Veil, Violet Burning

CYPRESS HILL

Hints of rap's growing fondness for marijuana go back to Tone-Loc's "Chiba, Chiba" and "Mean Green" in 1989-90. But these Latino rappers from L.A. are the real champions of the Cannibis cause. Their debut album had more references to marijuana (weed, grass, buddha, blunts) than any record since Cheech and Chong. It was featured on the cover of *High Times* magazine and they are the first group to be endorsed by NORML (the National Organization for the Reform of Marijuana Laws), surprising a few Grateful Dead fans!

They smoke large "joints" (or "blunts") on stage during their concerts. Their second album, *Black Sunday,* offers pro-pot praises like "Light Another" and "Stoned is the Way of Life." Rapper B-Real rationalizes his obsession this way: "I don't think of marijuana as a drug. Weed will never hurt anybody. Say no to crack, say no to heroin, to cocaine—those are drugs! But as far as weed goes, that's not a drug" (*Pulse,* 8/92). Get real, B-Real!

Did you ever notice that rockers and rappers are only against the drugs they don't use? They say no to drugs, unless they drink—then alcohol isn't really a drug. They say no to drugs, unless they smoke marijuana—and it's okay because it isn't a *dangerous* drug. This may all sound very high-minded to their young fans. The problems is, if their heroes are too busy doing lines to teach them to draw the line, their fans will cross the line every time.

Music Exchange: Cauzin' Efekt, D-Boy, Dynamic Twins, Grits, T-Bone

DANZIG

New Jersey native Glenn Danzig started out with a punk band called The Misfits in the late 1970s. They were one of a handful of gothic punk groups (e.g., The Damned, .45 Grave, Christian Death) that emphasized a demons-and-drama approach to their furious noise (sometimes referred to as death rock). Claiming that he was tired of the punk scene, Danzig disbanded the group in 1982 (there are those who suggest that he was frustrated by band members who had become unreliable because of their heroin use). Danzig's next band, Samhain (the pagan name for Halloween), lasted from 1984 to 1986. Danzig put his current band together in 1988. The music is a hard blues-rock style, and Danzig's vocals sound remarkably like Jim Morrison of the Doors. Albums include *Danzig* (1988), *Lucifuge* (1990) (the lyric sheet on the CD unfolds into an upside-down cross), *How the Gods Kill* (1992), *Thrall - Demonsweatlive* (1993), and the creatively titled *Danzig 4* (1994).

Danzig denies accusations that he's a practicing Satanist. He's a self-styled occultist who borrows his ideas from comic books, occult literature, and horror movies. He is obsessed with exploring the reasons for evil and the dark side of human nature. His song "Twist of Cain" proposes the "demon seed" theory that Cain sinned because he was the product of a sexual liaison between Satan and Eve (hence the term, 'evil').

Danzig presents a powerful and intimidating image to his fans. He has become like **Ozzy Osbourne** for the metalheads of the 1990s. He howls like a wolf and comes across like Conan the Rocker on his albums. He projects the mystique that he is something more than human and not quite of this world. But for all the menacing messages, Danzig offers nothing new. Paul had him pegged 2,000 years ago when he wrote: "For though they knew God, they did not honor God or give Him thanks. Instead they became futile in their speculations and their foolish heart was darkened. Professing to be wise, they became fools" (Rom. 1:21-22).

The DEAD KENNEDYS

Formed in the San Francisco area around 1977, DK was one of the most enduring and popular punk bands from the west coast. Their lyrics were a series of socio-political diatribes that challenged everything and offended everybody, making lead screamer Jello Biafra the perfect punk hero for thousands of angry, white suburban kids. His self-righteous ranting about the self-righteousness of the Moral Majority filled albums like *Fresh Fruit for Rotting Vegetables* (1980).

The cover of *In God We Trust* (1982) depicted Christ crucified on a $100 bill. *Frankenchrist* (1985) contained a poster by H.R. Giger (who created the artwork for *Aliens*) which was deemed obscene by the FBI. Biafra was actually arrested and tried for distributing pornography. The trials launched Biafra on a campaign against censorship and the PMRC (Parents' Music Resource Center). Although his legal battles broke the band up in 1987, Jello continues to be a punk on a mission. He runs an independent record company called Alternative Tentacles and publishes his own propaganda magazine on censorship and political anarchy. His post-DK music efforts are directed into a project called Lard, which he produces with Alain Jourgensen of **Ministry.** Biafra even ran for mayor in San Francisco (and came in fourth out of 13 candidates!).

Ironically, he found himself in a battle of another kind in May, 1994. Attending a show at the Gilman Street punk club (where **Green Day** got its start), Biafra was assaulted by punks who chanted "sell out" and "rock star" (*SPIN, 9/94*). He was beaten so severely he suffered a broken leg, extensive knee damage, and a head injury (*RS, 1/26/95*). But Biafra has never really given up his punk politics. His only crime is that he got older. Maybe now he'll start waking up to the way life really works: the middle-class and the Moral Majority aren't the ones who just don't "get it." It's the angry young men he inflamed with his music all these years. What was it that Paul said about reaping and sowing (Gal. 6:7-8)?

Music Exchange: the Blamed, Crashdog, Nobody Special

DEICIDE

This death metal band from Florida is perhaps the most serious satanic band on the scene. Lead screamer Glenn Benton advertises his allegiance to Satan with an upside-down cross, which he ritually brands into his forehead every third Sunday of the month. His songs are vivid descriptions of satanic sacrifices and hateful destruction, and concerts can become a minor bloodbath as Benton tosses raw meat and animal entrails to his fans. He's outspoken in his hatred for Christianity and claims to be destroying churches in Florida with Satanic curses. "My only beef is with God. I curse Him every day, because there is only one person who's responsible for the life I have to live and that's the bastard who created us. I f***ing hate Him! My belief system is with Satan" (*RIP*, 5/95).

> "**My** only beef is with God. I curse Him every day, because there is only one person who's responsible for the life I have to live and that's the bastard who created us. I hate Him!"
> – Glenn Benton of Deicide

While witnessing to metal fans outside a rock club in San Diego, I came face-to-face with Benton on Halloween Night in 1992. Trying to summon up his demons, he became so menacing and intimidating, he bordered on the psychotic. He threatened to suspend my soul in hell with a single word and destroy me with his bare hands. But when push came to shove, for all his intensity, he couldn't stand up to the truth of Christ, and I walked away unharmed.

Music Exchange: Living Sacrifice, Mortification, Paramecium

DEPECHE MODE

Formed in 1980, Depeche Mode (pronounced de-*pesh* mode; it's French for "fast fashion") was a major part of England's synthesized New Romantics movement. Although Vince Clark left the band in 1981, it was his song "People Are People" that opened the group up to the U.S.

in 1984. This humanist hit made them so popular, over 70,000 fans showed up for their concert in the Rose Bowl in 1988. (Clark went on to work with Allison Moyet in Yazoo (known as YAZ in America), and later with Andy Bell in the openly gay dance duo Erasure.) By 1994, they'd sold 15 million albums world wide (*LAT,* 8/23/95).

Time revealed a darker agenda and two major themes: kinky sex and nihilism. Songs like "Master and Servant" and "Black Dress" pointed to S&M and gay overtones—not to mention Martin Gore's penchant for wearing blue mascara, black fingernail polish, and black leather miniskirts. By *Music for the Masses* (1987) their message was clear: "(Singer David) Gahan's treatment of 'Strangelove,' a celebration of masochism, is a marvelous marriage of voice and material. For better or worse, he sounds as if he knows what he's talking about. Listen to this twice and you'll have a deeper understanding of masochists. Listen to it three times, and you'll be one" (*People,* 9/28/87).

The theme of nihilism is so prominent, they are sometimes referred to as Depressed Mood. It can be seen in songs like "World Full of Nothing" and "Fly on the Windscreen," which repeatedly proclaims: "*death is everywhere.*" They're both from the album *Dark Celebration* (1985), "which is undoubtedly the most desolate record they ever made" (*AMG,* pg. 100). So it wasn't altogether surprising to discover that Gahan, 33, tried to commit suicide in his West Hollywood home by slashing his wrists with a razor blade (*LAT,* 8/23/95).

They added to the despair by mocking God with "Blasphemous Rumors" (1984). "Personal Jesus," from the album *Violator* (1990), suggests that we should all just believe in whatever Christ makes us comfortable. The album *Songs of Love and Devotion* (1993) continued the controversy. Although there's a lot of religious imagery in the album, they seem to display more faith in sex than in God. Sexually experimental and spiritually empty, it's easy to see how Depeche Mode helped create the hopelessly dark moods which pervades Generation X today.

Music Exchange: Deitiphobia, Echoing Green, Painted Orange

DINOSAUR JR.

This alternative band has been hidden away in the obscure college-radio underground until recently. Starting as a punk band in Boston in 1983, they have become "the link between the post-punk rock of Hüsker Dü and the Replacements, and the grunge rock of the '90's" (*AMG,* pg. 102). They are often compared to Neil Young in his Crazy Horse days. Their music is mostly the product of drummer-turned-guitarist J. Mascis, who has a reputation for being painfully shy. "He writes most about the difficulties he has with dealing with the world outside his living room—especially with women, who interest him but make him nervous" (*SPIN*, 4/91). It's easy to see why his ramblings on loneliness and yearning appeal to so many introspective young men. But we can't afford to remain with Mascis' moods for long. Immobilized by self-doubt and overwhelmed by vague anxieties, there are nagging doubts that he will ever leave his room again. While we all need a hiding place from time to time, Christ calls us to face our fears (2 Tim. 1:7) and be more than conquerors (Rom. 8:37).

Music Exchange: Plankeye, Raspberry Jam, Starflyer 59, Villanelle

Dr. DRE. See N.W.A.

EAZY-E. See N.W.A.

EN VOGUE

This foursome was originally a girl-group called FM2, "constructed" by a couple of slick producers in San Francisco in 1988. Combining the glamour of '60s girls groups, the melody of '70s-style R&B, and the rhythms of '80s hip-hop, they have become the "funky divas" of the '90s. Visually, they project a sensual "look, but don't touch" tease that makes them perfect for MTV. The fact that they could actually sing (and not just breathe heavy) had some critics calling them the new Supremes and sent their songs up the white pop charts as fast as the black R&B charts. Hits like "Never Gonna Get It" and "Give Him Something He Can Feel" added to the image, and their appearance in **Salt-N-Pepa's** sexy "Whatta Man" video clinched it.

Behind the scenes, in personal interviews, the girls are much more down-to-earth. And they talk about God a lot: "God is good, and God is essential to this group. Without God, we'd be lost" (*RS*, 7/22/93). Like many R&B artists, there's so much discrepancy between their personal faith and their public image, it's hard to know what they really believe.

Music Exchange: Angie & Debbie (Winans), Nicole, Out of Eden

ENTOMBED

This Swedish death metal band originally called themselves Nihilist when they formed in 1987. Their first album, *Left Hand Path* (a reference to Satanism) in 1990 brought them critical approval as the best death metal band in Europe. Their second album, *Clandestine,* brought them to

America in 1991 on a tour with **Morbid Angel**. *Wolverine Blues* (1993) was marketed to a younger junior high crowd with a tie-in to Wolverine, the most popular character in the X-men comic book series. Members from this band have spawned two more death metal groups, Dismember and Unleashed.

While Entombed is becoming slightly more diverse musically, their lyrics reflect the same unholy scare tactics they started with. Songs like the blasphemous "Out of Hand," the brutal "Contempt," the wicked "Demon," and the chilling "Blood Song" (a tribute to Anne Rice's vampire novels) are sending kids screaming into the Pit. "Entombed set out to make as angry and brutal albums as they could, and they've succeeded on a frightening level" (*MM*, 4/94). There's nothing constructive here—just pure, brutal destruction and hatred.

Music Exchange: Crimson Thorn, Detritus, Mortification, Seventh Angel

ENIGMA

Technically, Enigma is not a band, but a studio project produced by Michael Cretu. The music is a unique blend of synthesized dance beats and music from ancient cultures (e.g., Gregorian or American Indian chants.) This dance hit sensation from Germany climbed to the top of the charts in 14 countries, before their album *MCMXC, A.D.* reached America in 1991.

The next album, *Cross of Changes* (1994), was more of the same although their spiritual bent was more obvious: "On Enigma's second album, their New Age tendencies come to the forefront, and occasionally obscure their captivating dance tracks" (*AMG*, pg. 117). "Sadeness" became Germany's biggest-selling single ever. It created a stir in this country, because many Americans had never heard Gregorian chant before and assumed it was some kind of satanic ritual. Actually, the focus of the song was sexual not satanic. The song is a dark homage to the Marquis de Sade, who was so brutal in his approach to sex, the term sado-masochism (S&M) is named after him. Cretu's wife, Sandra, contributes some mildly obscene lyrics to the album (in French, of course).

The solution to this Enigma lies in the only song on the first album with English lyrics. Sandra tells us in a breathy voice: "*The Principles of Lust are easy to understand / Do what you feel, feel to the end / The Principles of Lust are burned in your mind / Do what you want, do it 'til you're blind / Love....*" The infamous occultist, Aleister Crowley, put it more simply: "Do what thou wilt." Anton LaVey echoes the idea in *The Satanic Bible*: "Satanism represents indulgence instead of abstinence." This should be enough evidence for any Christian to explain the mystery behind this demented dance.

Music Exchange: the "Angels" project (Christi & Holli Banks), Scott Blackwell, Iona

ENYA

∙∙

Her real Irish/Gaelic name is Eithne Ni Bhraonain (no wonder she changed it!) She left the Irish folk group Clannad to record her debut album in 1986. Her second album, *Watermark* (1988), was enthusiastically received by the growing New Age music audience. Her third album, *Shepherd Moons* (1991), sold over 2 million copies, something of a phenomenon for this type of album.

Her music is everywhere now, in car commercials, movies like *Green Card, Far and Away, Toys,* and even on TV's "Baywatch"! She is sometimes referred to as a New Age artist, but that's simply a label the music industry uses to sell this style of music. She is actually deeply committed to her Irish Catholic roots. Her melodies are usually reverent, even solemn, like many old hymns. Her lyrics are often Gaelic (ancient Irish) or from the Latin Mass.

Enya appeals to young ladies who like the lovely, lilting feel of the music. Too much of today's modern rock (e.g., **Alanis Morrissette**) says that love is a cruel monster, lying in wait, ready to ambush and betray anyone foolish enough to reach out for it. Enya offers the quiet reassurance that love is a warm, wonderful thing to hope for. Our children should be encouraged to feel this way about love—whether it's from their parents, their future mates, or their Heavenly Father.

Music Exchange: the "Angels" project (Christi & Holli Banks), the Crossing, Iona, Jeff Johnson, Prayers and Worship project (Forefront)

Melissa ETHERIDGE

∙∙

This acoustic rocker emerged in the mid-1980s and went almost unnoticed amidst an avalanche of female artists emerging at the same time: Sinead O'Connor, Tracy Chapman, **Suzanne Vega**, Edie Brickell, Michelle Shocked, etc. Her first (self-titled) album (1988) won her a Grammy nomination, followed by *Brave and Crazy* (1989) and *Never Enough* (1992). Her most popular album, *Yes I Am* (1994), was a sly allusion to her sexual orientation. Her passionate rock about losing at love has earned her comparisons to Janis Joplin. The album, *Your Little Secret* (1995), continues the theme of frustrated relationships. "Her message: damn the doctors, destructive relationships are fun!" (*EW*, 11/17/95).

Following the lead of gay artists like **k.d. lang** and Janis Ian,

Etheridge went public about her lesbian lifestyle in 1993 at President Clinton's Inaugural Ball. She's now quite visible and vocal for gay issues. She was touted on the cover of one gay magazine as "Rock's Great Dyke Hope." She is already adept at parroting the lesbian myth: "A lesbian is the highest form of life....In the hierarchy of reincarnation, the lowest form is a heterosexual man. Then as you go up the ladder, the highest form is a lesbian" (*The Advocate*, 7/94). (Apparently, she isn't referring to Jacob's ladder.)

> "*A* lesbian is the highest form of life....In the hierarchy of reincarnation, the lowest form is a heterosexual man. Then as you go up the ladder, the highest form is a lesbian."
> — Melissa Etheridge

Like many lesbians, she sees Christianity as the great repressive enemy. "The religious right is so afraid of sexuality in general, and they hate the fact that we just have sex for sex—it's not just for procreation. So we must be just the evilest of evil, as far as they're concerned," she declared on the TV interview show "Charlie Rose" (7/11/94). This a misrepresentation of the Christian position. Homosexuality isn't wrong because Christians are afraid of gays. It's wrong because God says so.

Music Exchange: Margaret Becker, Ashley Cleveland, Andy Landis

EYEHATEGOD

This oppressive quintet was formed in New Orleans in 1988 with a sound that combines the anger of punk and the slow, dark sludgey sounds of **Black Sabbath.** Their first album included the tell-tale single "Man Is Too Ignorant to Exist." Then there was "Godson," their musical accompaniment to the insane ravings of Charles Manson.

What we have here are some angry artists who have chosen to focus on violence, addiction, slavery, self-mutilation, cruelty, abuse, and hate. They've been described as, "five men at the end of their world—at the death of faith and warmth" (*MM*, 3/93). The band explains itself this way: "It's because of our depressing surroundings that we've come to not care about anything. So we live off that vibe—promoting anger, frustration, and depression. We're screwing with society's head. We're preaching the End-time message" (*MM*, 3/93). It's terrifying to think about how many kids think these guys are cool, because they relate to this message. How do you offer hope to people who don't believe it exists?

Music Exchange: Crucified, Mortification, Oblation, Ritual

EXTREME
··

This Boston-based rock quartet plays a diverse fusion of musical styles from rock, rap, classical and jazz. They seem to be growing in a positive, spiritual direction with each new album. With two exceptions, the first album was filled with your typical hedonistic, heavy-metal hodgepodge. But the song "Rock a Bye, Bye" makes a remarkably strong pro-life statement for a secular rock group. And "Watching, Waiting" is a relatively reverent portrayal of the Crucifixion from the viewpoint of the thieves: *"Tears from my eyes that cannot see / He took the blame for me / So it shall be written / So it shall be done."*

The second album produced the warm love ballad "More Than Words," as well as an intriguing song called "Hole Hearted." The song would go well with C.S. Lewis' thoughts about how everybody has a God-shaped hole in their hearts: *"There's a hole in my heart / That can only by filled by you / Should have known from the start / I'd fall short with the things I do."* Mixed with these vaguely spiritual messages are some sinsational, sex-laden songs like "Wind Me Up," "Flesh and Blood," "Li'l Jack Horny," and "Suzi (Wants Her All-Day Sucker)".

The album *III Sides* presents yet another side of the band. It is a three-part album that devotes one side to politics and peace, another side to relationships (with women, family, and God), and a third side with a lushly-arranged suite produced with a 70-piece orchestra which asks questions about God's existence and the meaning of life.

Singer/songwriter Gary Cherone is an ex-Catholic who professes Christ without all the trappings of the institutional church. When asked who Christ was, Cherone responded "I would never deny Him three times or even once. He's the Son of God to me, period" (*HM*, 2-3/91). After that, he went on to talk about his favorite preacher, Chuck Swindoll.

This band is a mixed-bag that requires some song-by-song evaluation. They also require serious prayer. They are certainly moving in the right direction, but they are not a Christian band. Until they move to one Extreme or another, they will provide a good springboard for lots of lively discussions about rock and God in your home.

Music Exchange: Guardian, Holy Soldier, LoveWar

FAITH NO MORE

This is one of a handful of mostly West Coast bands (like Red Hot Chili Peppers, Soundgarden, and Primus) that redefined the boundaries of the hard rock/heavy metal scene. They started out as a raw punk band in San Francisco in 1982. In the early days, they went through a number of singers, and even **Courtney Love** sang for the band at one time. Their first two albums, *We Care A Lot* (1985) and *Introduce Yourself* (1987) were fronted by a frantic Chuck Mosely. His over-the-top anger and excessive alcohol use led to his being replaced by the demented stylings of Mike Patton (who also fronts a bizarre side-project known as Mr. Bungle).

The band gained national attention with 1989's *The Real Thing* and a single called "Epic," which received incessant airplay on MTV. The music was a unique blend of metal, funk, rap, and classical jazz. The lyrics are unique, too. Not many groups have written songs from the viewpoint of a vampire ("Surprise! You're Dead!"—a chilling portrayal of hell, if there ever was one) or a child molester ("Edge of the World"). The album eventually sold a million and a half copies.

But things seemed to unravel from there. *Angel Dust* (1992) was too experimental to hold the broad base of fans they had developed and only went gold. There was some controversy when it came out that keyboardist Roddy Bottom was openly gay. Infighting developed in the band, guitarist Jim Martin was kicked out, and the next album almost did not materialize. They finally released *King For A Day, Fool For A Lifetime* in 1995. Reflecting styles from thrash metal to lounge music, this album also seems to be too eclectic to sell well. All in all, the band seems to be losing the Faith and may soon simply be No More.

Fans point to the lyrics and music as creative and thought-provoking. So they should think about the spiritual perspective of a group that would choose a name like Faith No More and call their publishing company, Vomit God Music. Then there's Patton's favorite T-shirt displayed prominently on the cover of *Spin* magazine (12/90), which portrays multiple images of Christ masturbating in the Garden of Gethsemane. What is the underlying feeling/philosophy of the band? "We definitely rely heavily on bitterness for our creativeness. Bitter feelings, bitter times, bitter pills swallowed. . . .I don't see our music as that happy sounding at all" (*RIP*, 5/88). Even accounting for the tongue-in-cheek absurdism of the band, this group doesn't honor Christ in any way. Musical talent isn't enough to balance out blasphemy on the scales of universal justice.

Music Exchange: D. C. Talk (*Jesus Freak*), Don't Know, P.O.D. (Payable on Death), Precious Death

GIN BLOSSOMS

Alcohol is the predominant theme of this band. Their name is derived from a phrase used to describe the capillary damage seen in the nose and face that results from extensive drinking. The lyrics on their hit album *New Miserable Experience* (1993) look at life from the bloodshot eyes of an alcoholic. The writer of those lyrics (Doug Hopkins) was dismissed in 1992, before the album's release, because his drinking was out-of-control. Apparently in a depressive state about the band's success without him, Hopkins committed suicide, shooting himself in the head with a .38 caliber pistol in his home.

Musically, these depressive themes and circumstances are covered with a downright infectious roots-rock guitar sound reminiscent of the Byrds. As one critic put it, "With music as exhilarating as this, misery has rarely sounded so good" (*People,* 4/4/94). Yes, you too can learn to be happy about all the misery and hopelessness in this life! Anyone ready to drink to that?

Music Exchange: Black Eyed Sceva, Dime Store Prophets, Jars of Clay, Pray For Rain, Mike Roe (the 77's), This Train, Villanelle, the Waiting

GODFLESH

This British trio is named after an American Indian term for the drug peyote. Their music is a punishing and oppressive wall of noise that appeals to fans of both Black Sabbath's sludge-metal and Ministry's sterile synthesizer sounds. The band's central figure, Justin Broadrick, was raised by teenage parents in a drug-infested commune in England. His father was a heroin addict who tried to kill Broadrick several times before his mother divorced him. Broadrick started as the original drummer for

Napalm Death in 1985. He formed this band in 1988 with two other guys and a drum machine.

Their first album, *Streetcleaner* (1990), opens with the ramblings of serial killer Henry Lee Lucas (the subject of the documentary film *Henry, Portrait of a Serial Killer*—a popular flick among the *Faces of Death* fans.) Songs like "Wound" and "Might Trust Killers" from the album *Pure* (1992) only drive the darkness deeper. No wonder incidents occur at their concerts like the deadly disaster at the Country Club in Los Angeles in 1991, where several people were knifed and left bleeding in the parking lot while the band played on.

This band epitomizes the anguished death-wish mentality of so many industrial/grind-core/death metal bands today. Broadrick smokes tons of pot and does drugs to enhance his paranoia. The result is total emptiness: "I always look for hope in people and can't find any hope on any level. The only way out is pain for these people and all I see is horror" (*RIP*, 6/92). Justin has it all wrong, of course. The only Way out is to accept that Jesus paid the painful price already so that we can find hope and get on with our lives for Him.

Musical Exchange: Chatterbox, Circle of Dust

Amy GRANT

Amy was only 17 when her first album came out in 1977. Since then there have been more than 14 albums, 17 videos, 17 Doves, 5 Grammys, and 3 kids. This Tennessee doctor's daughter started writing songs to share with her church group when she was still in high school. A youth director named Brown Bannister heard her music and was impressed with her simple faith and sweet melodies. He found a way to get her songs on record and went on to produce many of her albums. Amy soon became a best-selling contemporary Christian artist with tunes like "Father's Eyes," "El Shaddai," "Thy Word," "Angels," "Lead Me On," "Sing Your Praise to the Lord," and "Ageless Medley" on albums like *Age to Age* (1982), *Unguarded* (1985), *The Collection* (1986), and *A Christmas Album* (1983), one of the best-selling Christmas albums ever.

Amy broke into the secular pop charts with "(Love Will) Find A Way" in 1985, followed by a duet with Peter Cetera (from the band Chicago) called "The Next Time I Fall (In Love)," which went to #1 in 1986. She's also had some success on the secular charts with songs like "Baby, Baby" (1992), "House of Love" (a duet with country artist Vince Gill) in 1994, and "Big Yellow Taxi" (a cover of Joni Mitchell's 1970 hit) in 1995. Amy's visibility has also been enhanced by interviews in *Rolling Stone*, hosting the video cable channel VH-1, and as a spokesperson for Target, especially during the Christmas season. You'll also find her sitting next to Mel Gibson, surrounded by many top country recording artists, in the video version of "Amazing Grace," the theme song for Gibson's film *Maverick* (1994), which was recorded in the loft of her barn.

Amy's crossover into secular music fostered a huge controversy in the church. As she catered more to the secular market, she was accused of selling out, losing her faith, and worse. It's true that her last few albums are not as clearly Christian as they once were, as her songs focused more on romantic love and social concerns like spouse abuse. However, she still manages to make her testimony clear somewhere on her albums (e.g., "Hope Set High" on *Heart In Motion*, 1991). Amy is a lovely Christian woman bringing a little salt and light into an otherwise dark music industry. She's having a positive impact on young people, as well as many artists in pop and country music. In light of confessions by Christian leaders lately of everything from adultery to embezzlement, the spiteful criticism directed at Amy seems a little overblown and unjustified. "Who are you to judge someone else's servant? To his own Master he stands or falls" (Rom. 14:4, NIV).

Music Exchange: Carolyn Arends, Gina, Cheri Keaggy, Crystal Lewis, Out of the Grey, Rebecca St. James, Tammy Trent

GRATEFUL DEAD
....

Named after an Egyptian ritual prayer, this psychedelic blues-rock band started as a jug band in the early '60s, calling themselves Warlock. They became the house band for the infamous Electric Kool-Aid Acid Test parties in the days when LSD was still legal. By 1966, the Grateful Dead were sitting dead in the middle of the flower-power revolution in the Haight-Ashbury district of San Francisco. Constant touring made them one of the most popular and profitable bands in America. Faithful fans, called Deadheads, followed them from one concert to another, year round. These rock-n-roll gypsies were turning parking lots into a carnival sideshow long before Lollapalooza became a fashionable rock festival.

The Dead have been linked with everything from the Rosicrucians to a cult called The Church of Unlimited Devotion (*CWR*, 4/92), but focus on the occult is misleading. What this band is about is *drugs*. It shows up in their lyrics and their lifestyle. They are involved in campaigns to legalize pot, and drugs are a primary topic in their fan magazine, *Relix*. This focus on drugs has had deadly consequences: three keyboard players have died in the band. "Pigpen" McKernan died in 1973 of liver failure associated with his alcoholism; Keith Godchaux died in a car accident in 1980; and Brent Mydland died in 1990, overdosing on a "speedball," a lethal combination of heroin and cocaine (*RS*, 9/20/90).

These tragedies are not restricted to the band. There's been a constant parade of reports of drug overdoses, drug-related deaths, even a homicide in 1989, at their concerts. The summer of 1995 proved to be the most disastrous. A riot involving 2,000 ticketless fans in Indianapolis took 200 police officers to subdue (*APN*, 7/4/95). The next morning two fans were found dead of drug overdoses. Two days later 100 people were injured, four of them critically, when the roof they were dancing on collapsed at a concert near St. Louis (*CDH*, 7/7/95). But the biggest blow to the band came when its leader Jerry Garcia died of a heart attack in August. Garcia, 53, was in a San Francisco-area drug rehabilitation facility undergoing treatment for heroin addiction at the time of his death (*SFC*, 8/10/95).

The idea that the long, strange trip may be over is devastating to Deadheads. "People need this to survive," said one young fan, "and they don't know what's going to happen to them if it ends" (*CT*, 7/10/95). People *need* this music to survive? That's a rather curious conclusion to come to about a lifestyle that's been killing fans and band members for thirty years. It's also potent evidence for the idea that some musical lifestyles can be as addicting and deadly as any drug.

Music Exchange: Lost Dogs

GREEN DAY
••

This San Francisco-area punk trio almost single-handedly sparked the revival of hardcore music in the '90s. Boyhood friends Billy Joe Anderson (guitarist/vocalist) and Mike Dirnt (his real name is Mike Pritchard, bassist) were both products of broken homes when they met. "I'd say we were as dysfunctional as a family could be," says Anderson's sister, "with the death of a father, a stepfather no one liked, and almost losing our mother at the same time" (*RS*, 1/26/95). They turned their anger and neglect into music, hammering out their aggressions in a punk club known as Gilman Street. After meeting drummer Tre Cool (Frank Edwin Wright III) in 1989, they asked him to join their band, which was originally called Sweet Children. They renamed the band (having a "green day" is slang for getting high on grass), and began to put out a few albums locally.

Their chart-topping album, *Dookie* (slang for "excrement"), was released in 1994. The album is full of the arrogant apathy and bored antagonism that characterizes so much of this music. This stoner/slacker philosophy comes out in songs like "Burnout" (*"I'm not growing up / I'm just burning out"*); "Chump" (*"I don't know you / But I think I HATE you"*);

"Coming Clean" (*"Seventeen and strung out on confusion"*); "Sassafras Roots" (*"I'm a waste like you / With nothing else to do"*); "Basket Case" (*"Do you have the time / To listen to me whine?"*), and "Longview," their ode to marijuana and masturbation: *"No time for motivation / Smoking my inspiration."* "They've got punk's snotty anti-values down cold: blame, self-pity, arrogant self-hatred, humor, and narcissism" (*RS*, 2/28/94).

It should come as no surprise that the boys in the band are all heavily into drugs and alcohol. "I think drinking and doing drugs are very important," says Dirnt (who was once described as a "giggly stoner" in *SPIN*, 5/94). "To me everybody should drop acid at least once." "I'm the guinea pig," boasts Tre Cool. "When people bring weed to our shows, that's wonderful. If somebody throws a bag of weed onstage, I dive right in." "I think I have a bit of an alcohol problem," confesses Armstrong. "I drink every day. I use it as a crutch to relax me. I'm not abusive, I just think I drink a little too much sometimes." Armstrong also admits to occasionally indulging in a practice common to underage punks at Gilman Street—chugging Robitussin. "People think that we're this big pot-smoking band, even though we sound like an amphetamine band," says Armstrong. "But I dabbled in a lot of speed for a long time. That was the drug of choice where I came from" (*RS*, 1/26/95).

> "*That's what rock-n-roll is for me, a kind of rebellious thing. It's getting away from authority figures, getting laid maybe, getting drunk, and doing drugs at some point."*
> — Slash of Guns N' Roses

Green Day's only concession to social consciousness has been to promote homosexuality to their young fans by having the blatantly gay punk band Pansy Division as the opening act on their 1994 tour. "There's a blatant spewing of homosexuality today and I think it's great," says Anderson. "I think it's the future of what's gonna happen to rock-n-roll music" (*PG*, 3/15/95). Their appearance at Woodstock in the summer of 1994 was a muddy affair—about 750 people broke their ankles in the mosh pit, Armstrong pulled his pants down on stage, and there was a huge melee in the mud in which Dirnt lost a couple of teeth. "It was the closest thing to chaos and complete anarchy that I have ever seen in my whole life," said Armstrong (*LAT*, 9/6/94). Their act is so disgusting even Armstrong's own mother has sent derogatory "hate" mail to him (*RS*, 1/26/95).

A concert in Boston in September, 1994 turned into a riot as 65,000 moshing fans battled police with mud, bottles, tear gas. The band egged the fans on from the stage, and Billy Joe was heard to scream, "The youth of Boston have finally taken over this f***ing city!" (*RS*, 11/3/94). In December, Armstrong delivered one tune stark naked during a concert at Madison Square Garden (*EW*, 12/23/94). "I never really thought that being obnoxious would get me where I am today," he admits (*RS*, 1/26/95). It's not hard to see why Green Day primarily appeals to adolescent and pre-adolescent boys. They think all this churning chaos and self-destruction is bloody good fun. "I've always thought that's part of our success," chuckles Dirnt. "We're immature" (*RIP*, 6/94).

The question here isn't whether the band is naughty or nice (a lawyer in Georgia is actually trying to have *Dookie* declared legally obscene, *AP*, 12/15/94). The question is, what are all the young fans learning from Green Day? "For a new generation of punks, the defining image of the music may no longer be Sid Vicious [of the **Sex Pistols**] puking in a New York hotel room, but Green Day singer Billie Joe shredding his sofa with a bread knife because there's nothing good on TV" (*SPIN*, 11/94). The message seems to be that aimless anger and violence, masturbation and zoning out on TV, happy homosexuality, denial through drugs and alcohol—it's all just good, clean American fun. It's what we all should aspire (expire?) to. Taking things one step further than the **Beastie Boys,** Green Day believes you should fight for your right to party—and for your right to be immature for the rest of your life. I don't think that's what Jesus meant when He said, "I have come that they may have life, and have it to the full (John 10:10b, *NIV*).

Music Exchange: Black Cherry Soda, Crashdog, MxPx, One Bad Pig

GREEN JELLY

This bizarre band was formed as a joke in Buffalo, New York in 1981. Originally called Green Jello, they were forced to change it when General Foods (the makers of Jello) threatened to sue them. More than 75 people have participated in the group, usually 8 to 10 at a time, with names like Moronic Dictator, Hotsy Menshot, Sadistica, and Jella Tin. Key members of the group moved to L.A. in 1986, where they found someone crazy enough to give them $60,000 for a video project. (This is really not enough money to make one good video. So they made 11 really bad ones.) When the video collection went gold, they decided it was time to make an actual record. Now there's talk of a TV show and a comic book.

They admit their music is dumb, and they use lots of props and sight-gags on stage to cover up how bad it all is. But their punk-edge pranks are going over with guys from junior high to college. Their Claymation video based on the story of the Three Little Pigs was a huge hit on MTV. The group is not as obnoxious and biting as **Gwar**, but they have more than their share of bathroom humor. Most of their act is simple, pointless foolishness. This is twinkie music (sugar and air—no substance) for a new generation of "airheads." As the warning on their video album states: "Go read a book, or you could end up like the idiots in this band!" It's a warning worth heeding.

Music Exchange: Blenderhead, Crashdog, Lust Control, MxPx (Magnified Plaid), One Bad Pig

GUNS 'N' ROSES
....

This hard-rocking band of bad boys formed in 1985, combining two club bands, Holly Rose and L.A. Guns, to become the house band for the Cat Club in Hollywood. Their first album, *Appetite For Destruction* (1987), featured some controversial cartoon cover art (a girl apparently molested by a robot) and sold over 9 million copies. It was still selling well when they released their second album, *Guns N' Roses Lies* (1989), two years later. Both albums wound up in the Top Five on the charts at the same time.

They seemed determined to bring the legendary excesses of The Who and The Rolling Stones into the 1980s. "We all have our problems," confessed bassist Duff "Rose" McKagan. "My problem is drinking. The same with (guitarist) Slash—he tends to drink way too much. Steve Adler (the drummer) just has a problem with everything, and we're trying to keep him from hurting himself" (*Thrasher*, 12/88). Singer Axl Rose, the son of a Pentecostal preacher from Indiana, collected guns and confessed to using heroin and cocaine, (*RIP*, 4/89). Slash created a furor by swearing on national TV during a speech at the American Music Awards in 1990. "That's what rock-n-roll is for me, a kind of rebellious thing," claimed Slash. "It's getting away from authority figures, getting laid maybe, getting drunk, doing drugs at some point. We are that kind of band" (*Musician*, 12/88).

Gradually, their appetite for destruction began to consume them, especially Axl. He became so paranoid, he sometimes refused to come out of his dressing room to perform his concerts. He got into fights with security personnel, promoters, and even his own fans. After living together for three years, he married model Erin Everly—the daughter of Don Everly (of the Everly Brothers) and the inspiration for the G'N'R song "Sweet Child of Mine." She filed for divorce less than a month later citing numerous incidents of physical abuse, bringing to mind a line from another G'N'R song, *"I used to love her / but I had to kill her"* (*People*, 5/21/90).

The band continued to put out albums like *Use Your Illusion I & II* (1991), and *The Spaghetti Incident* (1994), but things were obviously falling apart. Adler was fired for his heroin habit. Izzy went on to form the Ju Ju Hounds, while Slash formed Snakepit. Axl continues with new players, and the band is still popular in South America. But with the new surge of punk/hardore, they just aren't as popular in America as they once were. Axl doesn't appear to have learned anything from his past mistakes. We can only pray he will find a way to reach into his past, into his Christian roots, and get a fresh start for his future.

Music Exchange: Bride, Guardian

GWAR

This bizarre band combines performance-art punk with outer-space thrash to create a spaced-out rock opera for the demented. The group was started by a Virginia college theater arts group as a marketing experiment. It sold. Using a sci-fi theme of intergalactic warriors fighting over the planet Earth, Gwar uses bizarre costumes and as much filthy sex and bathroom behavior as possible to "entertain" their fans. Drinking toilet water and spraying the audience with green gunk from a two-foot plastic dildo are just some of the enlightening entertainment they offer their fans. And they offer total derision to anyone who's foolish enough to take them seriously. But seriously, folks, sometimes being gross and stupid just isn't that funny. And neither are these guys.

Music Exchange: Blenderhead, Lust Control, MxPx, One Bad Pig

P.J. HARVEY

Raised in the remote rural area of Dorset, England, Polly Jean Harvey always wanted to be a boy, wearing a crew cut and boy's clothes until she was 14. "When I was younger my mum wanted me to wear dresses," she confesses. "I'd wear them and sit and look sulky all day until I was allowed to put my trousers back on again. I was devastated when I started growing breasts. It was horrible. I didn't want them at all" (*SPIN*, 5/93). This tomboy grew up to be a critically-favored alternative artist, winning *Rolling Stone's* Songwriter of the Year award in 1992. She still struggles with resentment and resistance to her female condition in her music. On *Dry* (1992), she wrestles with everything from the unpleasant need for love to the burden of menstruation in songs like "Happy and Bleeding" and "Sheela-Na-Gig" (the Celtic goddess of sex and fertility).

Her next album, *Rid Of Me* (1993), went to the top of the college radio charts with songs about intimidating women ("50 Ft. Queenie") and being a man ("Man-Size"). The album *To Bring You My Love* (1995) is filled with confusing sexual/religious imagery as she grapples with desire and temptation in songs like "Snake" and the title tune: *"I was born in the desert / I've been down for years / Jesus come closer / I think my time is near....I've lain with the devil / Cursed God above / Forsaken heaven / To bring you my love."* Harvey has a genuine talent for articulating her frustration, but it's a senseless struggle. It's not her gender that has her feeling trapped, but her refusal to accept herself as God created her. She'll never be comfortable inside her own skin until she comes to terms with Him.

Music Exchange: Margaret Becker, Kim Hill

Juliana HATFIELD

Hatfield is another angst-ridden alternative artist along the lines of **Tori Amos, Liz Phair,** and **Belly**. Originally, she sang for the Boston-based pop band The Blake Babies from 1987 to 1991. Although romantically linked to Evan Dando of the **Lemonheads**, Hatfield claimed that she was still a virgin at 25 (*IV,* 8/92). Her first two solo albums (*Hey, Babe* and *Become What You Are,* both released in 1992) were college radio favorites, but not commercial successes. Her album *Only Everything* (1995) may change all that. With "songs about battles with eating disorders, self-mutilation, and other low self-esteem afflictions" (*EW,* 4/14/95), it's not surprising that she appeals primarily to the young female fans of "My So-Called Life," on which she had a guest role. Here's another performer who uses pop artistry to make hopeless confusion look attractive.

Music Exchange: Jan Krist, Riki Michelle, Julie Miller, Out of the Grey

HOLE. See Courtney LOVE.

HOOTIE AND THE BLOWFISH

This group has a unique composition for a rock band: the guitarist, bassist, and drummer are white, but the singer/songwriter, Darius Rucker, is black. They all met while attending the University of South Carolina in 1986. The band's name comes from combining the nicknames of two friends in the college choir (one had big owl eyes, the other had big Dizzie Gillespie jowls). After years of paying their dues, they signed to Atlantic Records and released *Cracked Rear View* in 1995 (the title comes from a line in a John Hiatt song). The music is a simple, melodic style with lots of acoustic guitar and lyrics that can actually be understood. The album sold 3 million copies in a matter of months.

Most of the songs are about personal relationships in terms that most everyone can relate to. Their first single, "Hold My Hand," is a pop-anthem love song which features the harmonies of David Crosby (of Crosby, Stills, Nash, & Young). "I'm Going Home" reflects Rucker's profound sadness over the death of his mother in 1992. "Only Want To Be With You" is an up-tempo love song, while "Let Her Cry" looks sadly at the break-up of a long-time relationship. Their only concession to social/political commentary comes with "Drowning," which decries the racism back home in South Carolina. "I always knew people were going to judge me," says Rucker, "because I was playing rock-n-roll with three white guys" (*RS,* 6/15/95).

For the most part Hootie music is honest and realistic. There's not much anger or angst here, or sexual sensationalism. Everyone in the band is a sports fanatic and they play a lot of golf and basketball. (Eventually, Rucker hopes to finish his degree in broadcast-journalism and be a sports commentator on ESPN). There are no sensational rock-star stunts and they seem to be basically drug-free. But while they're wholesome and unassuming by the world's standards, this is still not a Christian band. Their lyrics and interviews are marred by occasional cursing. They maintain the college party mentality, goofing off and getting drunk. Rucker has a child from a girlfriend he never married and is no longer dating. The music is enjoyable and relatable on the human level, but on the spiritual level, they still haven't found the Way home.

Music Exchange: Big Tent Revival, Dime Store Prophets, Third Day

Adina HOWARD

This new face on the R&B scene seems to be trying to out-sex **Salt-N-Pepa** and **T.L.C.** Howard, who started out singing in the church when she was seven, now proudly portrays her scantily-clad backside on her album *Do You Wanna Ride?* (which features the lyrics: *"Now baby come on and let's spend the night / We can do it all night until we get it right / Do you wanna ride?"*) Other songs feature such subtle come-ons as "You Got Me Humpin'" and "Horny For Your Love."

On her #2 gold single "Freak Like Me," she "proclaims the virtues of unconventional sex, boldly stating her preference for a 'roughneck' lover" (*LAT,* 5/7/95). (The term "freak" is a lyrical substitute in many of today's hip-hop/New Jack songs for the "F" word.) "I'm a '90s woman," explains Howard (who's 20). "I'm aggressive. There shouldn't be a double standard. Women can be just as aggressive as men" (*USA,* 5/9/95). Whatever happened to women trying to be as *spiritual* as men?

Music Exchange: Yolanda Adams, Out of Eden

HURRICANE

This black rapper started out hangin' with Run D.M.C., which led to his becoming the DJ for the Beastie Boys on the *Raising Hell* tour. Although he avoids the term "gansta rap," Hurricane's first solo effort, *The Hurra* (1995), is the same ol' hardcore hip-hop (a rap by any other name will smell as "street"). He raps about the benefits of getting high in "Get Blind" and depicts the violence of life on the streets in "Pass Me the

Gun." He defends the raps as reflections of his real-life experiences. "I had a crazy, crazy time growing up (in New York)—drinking and walking down the street with a gun in my pocket," says Hurricane, whose real name is Wendell Fite. "If you don't have a father to raise you, you find yourself doing some wild s***"(*RS,* 6/15/95). That much is certain. Without the guidance of the Father, you could find yourself raising hell forever.

Music Exchange: Gospel Ganstas, S.S. M.O.B., T-Bone

ICE CUBE. See N.W.A.

ICE-T

This West Coast ex-con is one of the most controversial rappers around. Tracy Marrow moved to Los Angeles as a teenager after his parents were killed in an auto accident. He survived the early years hustling as a gang member and reportedly did prison time. Inspired by the inner-city author Iceberg Slim, he started calling himself Ice-T. Doing what he called "crime rhyme," he released *Rhyme Pays* in 1987. The album was filled with violent images ("Pain," "Squeeze the Trigger") and lurid sexuality ("Sex," "I Love the Ladies"), bringing us gansta rap two years before **N.W.A.** released *Straight Outta Compton*. He followed that up by writing the title song for the graphic gang movie *Colors* in 1988.

> **"My** message is: Go to school, don't end up in jail, drugs ain't gonna help you."
> — Ice-T

On *The Iceberg (Freedom of Speech— Just Watch What You Say)* (1989) he took on censorship and included one of Jello Biafra's diatribes on the topic. His first acting role was playing an undercover cop in the film *New Jack City* (1991). *O.G. Original Gansta* (1991) introduced his new project—a heavy metal band called Body Count. His album with this group in 1992 included the explosive song "Cop Killer." It became even more controversial than N.W.A.'s "F*** the Police" (1989), as people backed police in a threatened boycott of Time-Warner products. Ice-T pulled the song off the album, but performed it at every show on the Lollapalooza tour that summer. After this incident, Ice-T's rap career declined. A muddled effort called *Home Invasion* (1993) was not well-received, but he stays visible in movies like *Trespass* (with

Ice Cube in 1993) and *Tank Girl* (1995), and a recurring role on TV's "New York Undercover".

Ice-T says he's "a negative role model with a positive message" (*BB*, 7/91). Unlike other gansta rappers, he's always been up front about the downside of gang life. "My message is: Go to school, don't end up in jail, drugs ain't gonna help you" (*BILL*, 6/8/91). He seems to be drug- and alcohol-free and has been married to the same woman for over ten years. He excuses his violent and obscene imagery this way: "You have to get someone's attention before you can get a message across. Telling kids, don't do it, doesn't work. What good is a message song if you can't get people to listen?" (*R&B*, 12/89); and "Adolescents are an unconventional enemy, and it takes unconventional tactics" (*Parade*, 8/12/90). Deadly calls to cop killing will cancel any good he might otherwise do, but the main fallacy in his logic is assuming kids *see* the substance underneath the sensationalism, much less value it. Most of his fans are too busy trying to be cool to go much deeper. Just because Ice-T is sincere in his efforts, doesn't mean he's going to be successful. There are better ways to beat the bullet than by burying yourself in crime rhymes.

Music Exchange: Gospel Ganstas, S.F.C., S.S. M.O.B., T-Bone, XL and DBD

Janet JACKSON

Competing with eight talented brothers and sisters in the famous Jackson family, Janet has carved out a name for herself in dance music that is second only to her brother Michael. By the time she was seven (1973), she was performing with her older brothers in the Jackson 5. At the age of ten (1976) she was acting in the TV series "Good Times," and later appeared on "Diff'rent Strokes" and the TV version of "Fame." For awhile, her life and career seemed to stall. Her first two albums, *Janet Jackson* (1982) and *Dream Street* (1984), were not very successful. Her secret marriage to James Debarge in 1984 (she was 17) was annulled after seven months. In 1985, she hooked up with the successful production team of Jimmy Jamm and Terry Lewis, and Janet finally got *Control* (1986)—an album which topped the charts, produced five Top 10 hits, and sold 4 million copies. The follow-up album *Rhythm Nation 1814* (1989) was even bigger, spawning seven Top 10 hits.

In 1991, she got a contract for $40 million for her next three records. It's ironic that she signed with Virgin Records, in light of the very un-virgin material on the album *janet* (1993). The first single, "That's the Way Love Goes" is about sex, not love: *"Reach out and feel my body / I'm gonna give you all my love."* "You Want This" teases a young man with sex that he can't have (but gets anyway). She does her best Donna Summer moan on "The Body That Loves You": *"Stroke me so gently my love / I love it when you mmmmm / I love it when you release my desire."* "If" is a celebration of oral sex and "Any Time, Any Place" proposes sex in public places, which seems to be the top turn-on for the twenty-something crowd these days (*USA*, 5/3/93). Revealing costumes and sexually-explicit dancing at her concerts brings those themes to life for her young audiences. "I love feeling deeply sexual," she says now, "and I don't mind letting the world know" (*RS*, 9/16/93).

We've come to expect this from Madonna, but Janet's always had a more wholesome image. She's not just a cute pop star anymore. "Janet's act used to be cute and bubblegum. Now it's a potboiler, with Janet strutting and shaking her butt and singing songs that are furiously sexual" (*SPIN*, 1/87). You may need to discuss a couple of key question with your family: Why does the music industry insist on pushing all its young artists into singing about sex? And why are the sexual fantasies on *janet* considered more "adult" than the social/political themes addressed on *Rhythm Nation*? Why do they describe the album as sensual, but not sexual; suggestive, but not explicit? Do they even know the difference? Is there any difference anymore? Be prepared for some lively answers from your children.

Music Exchange: Angie & Debbie (Winans), Lisa Bevill, Kim Boyce, Gina, Nicole, Out of Eden, Tammy Trent

Michael JACKSON

From his earliest accolades as a child star to the latest accusations as a child molester, Michael Jackson has been dancing in the show business spotlight for over 25 years. At the age of 10, he joined his brothers Jackie, Tito, Marlon, and Jermaine to become the Jackson 5. Signed to Motown Records in 1969, they became the biggest black pop/soul vocal group in the business, selling over 100 million records. Michael quickly took center stage as the group's cute, pre-teen singer and was soon recording solo albums along with his group efforts. His first #1 solo hit, "Ben" (1972), was a sentimental ode to a rat—an eerie prelude to the many oddities that would fill Jackson's career. In 1978, he played the Scarecrow to Diana Ross' Dorothy in *The Wiz,* a funky musical update of *The Wizard of Oz.* During the filming, Jackson met Quincy Jones who would produce the music that made him a superstar in the '80s. Their first project together, *Off The Wall* (1979), had four hit singles and sold over 9 million copies. His success also bolstered his brothers' new project (now known simply as the Jacksons), on their *Triumph* tour in 1981.

His *Thriller* album (1982) became the biggest album of all time, selling over 43 million copies worldwide! Its wide variety of musical influences included a duet with Paul McCartney and the driving guitar of Eddie Van Halen. Jackson also made good use of a relatively new music phenomenon known as MTV. "Billie Jean" was the first "black music" video to break big on the music channel, and "Beat It" became one of its all-time most popular videos (inspiring the food-obsessed parody "Eat It," which put **"Weird Al" Yankovic** on the music map). The video for the title tune was an elaborate mini-movie with a horror theme, spawning a successful video of the video, *The Making of Thriller.*

For awhile, it seemed as if Michael Jackson could do no wrong. The world watched in wonder as he moonwalked across the stage at Motown's 25th Anniversary Celebration in 1983. He was nominated for an unprecedented 12 Grammys in 1984, and won 8. He outbid Paul McCartney for the **Beatle's** catalogue (some 260 songs) in 1985, paying more than $45 million. Inspired by Band Aid's relief efforts for starving children, he joined forces with Quincy Jones and Lionel Richie in 1985 to produce the "We are the World" video, which became the biggest selling single up to that time. He produced a short science-fiction film called "Captain EO" in 1986, which became a major attraction at Disneyland. He became a best-selling author in 1988 with his autobiography *Moonwalk*, which was turned into a movie, *Moonwalker*, later that year.

Even his "Bad" moves seemed more savvy and successful than most. After their less-than-victorious *Victory* tour in 1984, he left the Jacksons, effectively dissolving the group. His $10 million contract to endorse Pepsi-Cola in 1986 almost lost its fizz when his hair caught on fire while filming the first commercial. (Jackson still won't drink Pepsi to this day.) He will probably never top the success of *Thriller*, but his long-awaited follow-up album *Bad* (1987) did very well by normal pop standards, topping the charts in 25 countries and selling a more-than-respectable 6 million copies in the U.S. alone. Switching to producer Teddy Riley for a hipper, new jack feel, Jackson did nearly as well with *Dangerous* (1991). The video for "Black and White" debuted on national TV, and featured his friend Macaulay Culkin (of *Home Alone*) and a new film technique called "morphing." The 11-minute montage closed with a dark segment involving a panther, some wind, screaming, smashing car windows, and some frantic dancing with lots of zipping and unzipping—leaving the world scratching their heads. Were we watching an entertainment genius or an eccentric madman? Perhaps, a bit of both.

While Jackson had a firm grip on the music world, his grasp of reality seemed more uncertain. He began to reshape himself through plastic surgery—efforts which seemed bent on obscuring his most distinctive black and masculine features. There was the inexplicable oddity of wearing one white glove. The tabloids were filled with rumors that he was sleeping in a hyperbaric chamber (an expensive oxygen tent) in a effort to prolong his lifespan. A morbid fascination with the bones of the Elephant Man in England reportedly led to a $100,000 bid to purchase them. He retreated into a child's fantasy world of his own making, filling his California ranch with games, rides, exotic animals, and children invited for sleep-overs. For awhile, his best friend seemed to be a chimp named Bubbles.

Jackson is trying to get back on track with a two-album package of new tunes and old hits called *HIStory* (1995). The new songs are full of angry accusations (lots of F- and S-words). There is also an unhealthy dose of victimized self-pity that seems incongruent with the King-sized ego of someone who insists the music world address him as "The King of Pop." There's a promo film featuring goose-stepping soldiers, frantically faithful fans, and the dramatic unveiling of a 50-foot statue of Jackson (which ironically seems to be made of plastic.) One reviewer called it "the most boldly vainglorious self-deification any pop singer ever undertook with a straight face" (*SDU*,6/16/95). High visibility for the project included a shallow "in-depth" interview with Diane Sawyer (6/95), but the album did not sell as well as was hoped.

Jackson may not be generating as much interest in his music as he once did, but he still generates a great deal of speculation about everything from his sexuality to his spirituality. Despite concerted efforts to appear in public with sexy beauties like Brooke Shields and Madonna, he's never been able to shake speculations that he is gay. Even his marriage to Elvis Presley's daughter, Lisa Marie, in 1994 did not put the matter to bed. Cynics see it as a contrived attempt to divert attention from the much-publicized charges of child molestation. Despite an out-of-court settlement with an alleged victim (reportedly in the $20 million range), the issue has never been firmly resolved and accusations continue. Spiritually, he reflects a vague and undefined New Age idealism. Although he renounced his parents' religion (Jehovah's Witnesses), one wonders what impact his wife's religious affiliation (the Church of Scientology) might have on his future and his finances.

When all is said and done, the key to Jackson's confusing character may simply boil down to "Black and White." To begin with Michael's motivations for the calculated changes in his appearance may be more than just skin deep. "Michael Jackson has spent most of the last decade gradually stripping himself of the trappings of his former identity, trying to transform himself into a superstar Everyman" (*LAT*, 11/24/91). Erasing these distinctives seems to be his way of identifying with everyone, regardless of color, sex, or creed. But in trying to be all things to all men, Jackson has become a cultural icon at the expense of his personal identity. This can be deadly to a pop music career, because fans aren't loyal to a public image unless they find a deeper emotional identity they can relate to.

At an even deeper level, Jackson struggles with his spiritual identity. Is he Black or White, Good or Bad, Beauty or Beast? Is he the white knight (in a white T-shirt) in his video—an altruistic beauty with high ideals? Or is he the black beast (the panther within), breaking out into uncontrolled violence and sexual frenzy without warning? He wants to express his enlightened side, but what does he do with his dark side? Jackson wants to save of the world, but he fears he can't even save himself. He ought to write about *that* struggle; it's one we can all relate to. The apostle Paul understood the struggle well: "I do not understand what I do. For I have the desire to do what is good, but I cannot carry it out. For what I do is not the good I want to do. No! The evil I do *not* want to do—*this* I keep doing. What a wretched man I am! Who will rescue me from this body of death? Thanks be to God—through Jesus Christ, our Lord!" (Rom. 7:15, 18-19, 24-25, NIV) Ultimately, even the King of Pop must come to terms with the King of Kings, if he is going to resolve the deep dilemma in his soul.

Music Exchange: Troy Johnson, Ji Lim, Gary Valenciano

JANE'S ADDICTION. See PORNO FOR PYROS.

JODECI

This Charlotte, North Carolina, quartet grew quite popular with their mix of R&B soul and hip-hop styles known as New Jack Swing. The group is composed of two sets of brothers, **Jojo** (Joel) and **K-Ci** (Cedric) Hailey and Dalvin and DeVante **De**Grante (parts of their names go together to form Jo-De-Ci). Their first album, *Forever My Lady* (1991), had several chart-topping ballads and put them on a par with the popularity of **Boys II Men.**

But time has changed the focus and appeal of their music. *Diary of a Mad Band* (1993) evidenced a turn toward from romantic ballads to "a string of innuendo-laden come-on numbers, complete with explicit language, tired raps and samples, and the kind of sentiments and appeal better suited to a *Penthouse Forum* entry than an album" *(AMG,* 1994, pg. 177). Their latest album, *The Show, The After-Party, The Hotel* (1995), continues the trend with raunchy tunes like "Room 577" (an ode to pornography), "Fun 2 Nite" (multiple sex partners) "Pump It Back" (just sex) and "Freek'N You" (*"I don't give a d*** about nothing else / Freek'n you is all I need / Tonight I need your body"*—more sex!)

These boys do have religious roots. The Degrates' father is the pastor of a Pentecostal Holiness church in Charlotte, and they cut their musical teeth on gospel music contests. But they've taken a turn away from that since they got into the business. They dress more like gangsta rappers than choir boys. There are alarming reports of sexual harassment of the young extras on their videos, including charges that they sexually assaulted an 18-year-old girl at gunpoint (*Vibe,* 12/93). There is little evidence that their spiritual inheritance influences much of their lives today. These boys' own parents won't listen to their music, and that's probably a clue as to what any Christian's response should be.

Music Exchange: Church of Rhythm, Dawkins & Dawkins, LaMore, Soul Tempo

Montell JORDAN

Jordan is another black artist taking R&B from the romantically seductive to the sexually graphic. The 6'8" Compton, California, native graduated from Pepperdine University and got a record contract with Def Jam through a contact with Russell Simmons (Run-D.M.C.). He's also a graduate of **R. Kelly's** school of bump 'n' grind. His album *This Is How We Do It* (1995) features such subtle tunes as "Down On My Knees," "Somethin' 4 Da Honeyz," and "I Wanna Get Laid" (*"We don't have to be lovers / We don't have to be friends / I just wanna see you naked in the raw"*). The first hit single (the title cut from the album) is actually the tamest cut on the whole album—which, of course, gets the kids to buy the album thinking it's pretty safe.

What's puzzling about his choice of songs is that Jordan came from a healthy, in-tact family and grew up in the church. In fact, he was director of the Carver Missionary Baptist Church choir when he was only 14 (*People*, 6/19/95). You'd think he'd have more to sing about than just repeating every adolescent make-out line in the book. Maybe he needs to go back to reading The Book.

Music Exchange: Dawkins & Dawkins, LaMore

R. KELLY
∙∙∙

Growing up on Chicago's South Side, Robert Kelly was raised on church music, but he performs some of the most sexually graphic R&B on the charts today. His second album is called *12 Play* (1993), a word-play that means 3 x *fore*play. It went to #1 on the R&B charts and hit the Top 10 on the mainstream pop charts with sexual tunes like "Your Body's Callin' " and "I Like the Crotch on You." To say the hit single "Sex Me" is steamy is an understatement. But Kelly just laughs it off, saying, "This is the clean version—you should have heard it before the cuts!" (*LAT,*1/9/94). His music is so popular, he's said to have singlehandedly changed R&B from soft seduction to sexual raunch (*USA*, 5/9/95).

Despite lyrics to the contrary, Kelly claims his music is basically Christian. He cites his work on the Winan's album *All Out* (1993) and says, "My show is pretty much gospel, just the lyrics are the opposite way. When I'm singing '12 Play,' I feel the spirit of God" (*USA*, 4/19/94). Like many black singers raised in the church, Kelly believes that simply having gone to church is what makes him spiritual. Anyone can claim to be a Christian, but Jesus teaches us to examine the fruit of our lives (Matt. 7:15-23).

Kelly may *feel* inspired by God, but it is what he inspires in others that really tells the tale. Recognized in a shopping mall, a teenage fan started screaming that she had to "do something" for him. She took her panties off right there in the mall and threw them to him (*DFP*, 1/31/94). If Kelly can elicit this kind of public behavior, just think what kids will be inspired to do in private!

Music Exchange: Church of Rhythm, Mike E., Idol King, Washington

KING DIAMOND

Kim Petersen is a former soccer star from Denmark, who gave it all up to become a heavy metal howler named King Diamond. Claiming to have lived in a haunted apartment in his native Copenhagen, Petersen began a serious study of the occult. He gave up soccer and a part-time gig with a band called Black Rose to join Mercyful Fate in 1981. The band was blatantly satanic (with lyrics like: "*I deny Christ, the Deceiver*"), and the stage shows were straight from **Alice Cooper's** school of Shock Rock. His microphone stand is made of human leg bones formed into an upside-down cross. He has anointed his audiences with blood, sacrificed dolls filled with pig's entrails, and has held black masses after his concerts. They garnered a large cult following in Europe but were too weird to find an American audience at the time. After two albums with Mercyful Fate, he went solo in 1985.

Albums like *Abigail* (1987), *Them* (1988), and *The Eye* (1990) took a more oblique occult approach—concept albums about ghosts and haunting that got him a larger American audience. Moving to Dallas, Texas, in 1992, he released some original demos on an album called *Return of the Vampire* and began performing with a re"vamped" version of Mercyful Fate. A nationwide tour in 1993 met with fair success among the growing number of death metal fans here. In 1995, he released *Time* with Mercyful Fate and *The Spider's Lullaby* as King Diamond.

While many metal bands have used Satanism as a sales gimmick, King Diamond is one of the few artists who openly professes to be a practicing Satanist (besides Glenn Benton of **Deicide**). But like many who have truly studied the occult, King Diamond rejects the hackneyed horror-movie concepts of sacrificing babies to a red devil with horns. Instead, he echoes Anton LaVey's philosophy (as cited in the *Satanic Bible*) with subtle clarity: "Satanism isn't dangerous at all. It's a sound life philosophy. It says carry out your feelings, have a good life, enjoy yourself while you're here. You don't know what comes after, so why not get the most out of the here and now" (*NM*, 6/85). That may make sense to many kids, until they understand what Christ says: "If anyone wishes to come after Me, let him deny himself and take up his cross and follow Me. For what will a man be profited if he gains the whole world and forfeits his soul? What will a man give in exchange for his soul?" (Matt. 16:24, NAS). One of these Kings is an imposter.

Music Exchange: Living Sacrifice, Tourniquet (first album)

KISS

This is one of the "initial" rock-n-roll bands said to have secret satanic roots. For years Christians have contended that KISS stands for **K**ings, **K**nights, or **K**ids **I**n **S**atan's **S**ervice. There is no evidence for this, but the band allowed these rumors to continue to enhance their image. It made them seem more dangerous, more mysterious, and made them more popular, thus enabling them to sell many more albums. The truth about the band is less spooky, but no less sinful.

Gene Klein was born in Israel of Hungarian-Jewish parents who moved to New York when he was 9. Klein finished college and began a career as a school teacher. Feeling trapped teaching fifth and sixth graders, he changed his name to Simmons and began searching for a new life in rock-n-roll. He formed an unsuccessful bar band called Wicked Lester with guitarist Paul Stanley (real name: Paul Eisen) in 1970. After recruiting new musicians in drummer Peter Criss (Peter Crisscoula) and guitarist Paul "Ace" Frehley in 1972, they decided to rename the band and try a new image. Singer/bassist Simmons suggested calling the band "F***," but they realized they'd never get an album contract with a name like that. Stanley suggested the next best thing, KISS. "KISS can be taken in all sorts of ways," asserts Simmons. "KISS could be the kiss of death. It's sexual, it's soft. It could certainly be hard—'kiss off' or 'kiss this.' You can use it in all sorts of ways, and we often do" (*HRV*, 12/8/85).

KISS' music was a crude, bombastic form of hard rock that would come to be called heavy metal. But it was their unique appearance and outlandish stage shows that got them noticed. Along with **Alice Cooper's** shock-rock shows, KISS put on some of the most elaborate rock concerts of the '70's. These leather-clad lunatics used their "spooky kabuki" make-up to bring comic book fantasies to life. Simmon's bat-persona became a blood-drooling, fire-spitting demon, but he is equally famous for his obscenely long tongue. Unpredictable near-disasters like Simmons accidentally setting his hair on fire (on at least three separate occasions) only enhanced his mystique.

Stanley was the "star child," Criss was the "cat man," and "Space Ace" Frehley was supposed to be the "out-of-this-world alien." Their fans, known as the KISS Army, began to flock to shows dressed and made up just like the band. Their stage persona was enhanced by publicity stunts like the 1977 KISS comic book produced by Marvel, which reportedly mixed real blood from the band members into the red ink (*RSE*, pg. 310). There was also a movie called *KISS Meets the Phantom of the Park* in 1978.

Musically, they weren't an immediate success. Early albums (*KISS*, 1974; *Hotter Than Hell*, 1974; *Dressed To Kill*, 1975) met with small sales and no radio play. It was their live album, *Alive!* (1975), that put them over the top, eventually selling 4 million copies. This was followed by

Destroyer (1976) and *Love Gun* (1977), a series of mediocre solo albums in the late 1970s, and a bewildering concept album called *The Elder* in 1981. Peter Criss left the band in 1980 and Ace Frehley left in 1982 to form Frehley's Comets. Although band members had not been seen or photographed without their makeup for ten years, it finally came off in 1983 for MTV.

What followed was a series of blatantly sexual albums like *Lick It Up* (1983), *Animalize* (1984), and *Crazy Nights* (1987), perfectly timed for the burgeoning glam metal movement. Altogether they produced 25 albums in their 20-plus years, 12 of them going platinum, and they're not done yet. Over the years, it's gradually become apparent just what an enormous influence KISS has been in shaping the look and feel of rock-n-roll. Nowhere is that more apparent than on their recent tribute album called *KISS My Ass* (1994), which includes artists as diverse as **Garth Brooks, Nine Inch Nails,** and **Dinosaur Jr.**, all of whom had been part of the KISS army as kids.

Despite the demonic implications in the early incarnation of KISS, this band has always been primarily about sex. Gene Simmons repeatedly says that everyone gets into rock music for sex and anyone who denies that is lying. Paul Stanley claims to have over 2,000 Polaroid photos of the groupies he's slept with (*NW,* 4/18/88). Songs like "Love Gun," "Lick It Up," and "Uh, All Night" are more than suggestive. They encourage their fans to live out these fantasies at their concerts: "Filling the gaps (between songs) are embarrassing and shameful attempts by Paul Stanley to titillate the mostly high school-aged audience by telling explicit sexual stories. Just before the groups vulgar 'Lick It Up,' he directed a spotlight to shine on several young females near the stage whom he had successfully encouraged to expose themselves" (*Kansas City Times,* 2/88). With this band, you don't have to look for secret codes or hidden meanings. Their sex-and-party message contradicts the teachings of Christ in ways that are obvious even to the most naive child.

Music Exchange: Shout, Whitecross, X-Sinner

L7

This all-female punk band was formed in Hollywood in 1987. The name refers to an old '50s expression for being square (put the "L" and the "7" together). Their distinctive look includes tattoos (of power tools!), nose and navel rings, and some unique hair colors. Their earlier albums, *L7* (1987) and *Smell The Magic* (1990), were released on **Bad Religion's** independent label, Epitaph. The album *Bricks Are Heavy* (1992) featured the cynical Riot Grrrls anthem, "Pretend We're Dead." They founded Rock for Choice, an organization designed to produce records and promote benefit concerts for the pro-abortion movement. They won a Feminist of the Year award in 1992 from the Feminist Majority Foundation for their efforts. Their first adventure on film was to pose as a punk band called Camel Lips in the movie *Serial Mom* (1994).

Like many hardcore bands, L7 tends to be politically and socially-conscious, as well as personally angry and vindictive. There are no love songs here, no sexual come-ons, but there are songs about abortion, smoking marijuana, and feminine hygiene. This is punk rock with feminist overtones. Singer Donita Sparks claims it's due to her upbringing: "My mom would take me to ERA marches. My parents taught me that getting an education was more important than getting a husband. They were very open-minded" (*CT,* 8/10/92).

Despite this, they claim they're not really committed to the feminist agenda: "It's hard for us to carry the baggage of a political agenda," says bass player Jennifer Finch, "when all we ever wanted to do was go on the road, do some drugs, play some rock, and have some sex" (*BAM,* 9/9/94). Whether they're willing to own it or not, they have become a voice for women who feel they need to be tougher and cruder than men in order to protect themselves in an abusive world. But becoming just like the men they hate is no solution. Women can't become all that God created them to be if they keep trying to be something they're not.

Music Exchange: the Clergy, Morella's Forest, Ordained Fate, Plague of Ethyls

k. d. lang

Katherine Dawn Lang was born (1962) and raised in Alberta, Canada. Her love for Patsy Cline led her to form the country band the Reclines in 1983. But her performance art background gave her music a strange kick that wasn't strictly country. "Lang's frantic stage manner and odd cowgirl look (spiky hair, sawed-off boots, Western shirts, and torn stockings) have led to such descriptions as 'punkabilly' and 'the prairie princess' of cow punk" (*LAT,* 3/7/87).

Her first album, *Angel With A Lariat* (1987), was a raucous rockabilly romp, but it didn't receive as much attention as her duet with Roy Orbison covering his classic tune "Crying." *Shadowland* (1988) demonstrates a smoother, smokier style she dubbed "torch and twang." *Absolute Torch and Twang* (1989) mixed some bouncing band tunes with soaring solos. Although nominated for three Grammys, America's heartland never really embraced her quirky, left-of-center persona. lang made no bones about being a vegetarian, and she really gave cowboys something to beef about with her "don't eat meat" promo for the extremist animal rights group PETA (People for the Ethical Treatment of Animals) in 1990.

But lang was changing more than her musical direction. A video for "Trail of Broken Hearts" depicted lang conjuring a vision of a sensual feminine spirit: "This just may be country's first mainstream homoerotic music video" (*EW,* 2/8/91). By 1992, she publicly acknowledged her lesbian lifestyle. Her biography (*k.d. lang: All You Get Is Me,* 1994) says she "may have been the key to unlocking the closet door for the entire pop music industry," implying that lang's outing gave David Geffen, **Melissa Etheridge**, and Janis Ian the courage to come out. She certainly began to draw a larger lesbian audience to her concerts: "In some instances, it gets a little crazy," lang confesses. "Sort of like a lesbian Beatlemania" (*People,* 3/8/93).

"You've had an interesting career when you get into more trouble for advocating vegetarianism than for announcing you're a lesbian" (*EW,* 12/93). Her open homosexuality seems to have actually bolstered her career. *Ingenue* (1992) gave her a Grammy-winning hit in "Constant Craving." Her appearance with Tony Bennett on his MTV "Unplugged" special in 1993 helped revived his career. "Back when Bennett ruled the charts, who would have predicted that some day his duet with a Canadian lesbian vegetarian country recording artist might be a wise career move?" (*EW,* 2/17/95). Who, indeed? It *is* a strange world we live in, but remember, we're to be strangers to this kind of strangeness (Exod. 2:22, 18:3; Heb. 11:13-14; cf., Rom. 1:22-32; 1 Cor. 6:9-10; and 2 Tim. 3:1-7).

Music Exchange: Susan Ashton, Ashley Cleveland, Kim Hill, Andy Landis

LEMONHEADS

This Boston-based trio began as a punk rock band in 1986. They got on the radio with a cover of Suzanne Vega's "Luka" and later with a loopy version of Simon and Garfunkle's "Mrs. Robinson." In 1990, most of the band ended up at Harvard, while singer Evan Dando ended up drugged out and depressed in Australia. It took a little help from friends like actor Johnny Depp and singer Juliana Hatfield to get him back on his feet. *It's A Shame About Ray* (1992) demonstrated Dando's new melodic folk/pop direction. His camera-ready good looks earned him a spot as one of "The 50 Most Beautiful People in the World" (*People,* 6/93). The band became an MTV staple with 1994's *Come On, Feel the Lemonheads* (a play on Slade's *Cum On, Feel the Noise,* 1984).

Despite his rock-hunk appearance, Dando is more like a spaced-out '60s reject. He rambles aimlessly in interviews, rarely answering the questions put to him. His songs often focus on the insignificant details of life, like how the water goes down the drain backwards in Australia—sort of a Seinfeld of songwriting. But there is a dark underbelly to this harmless, hippie persona. To start with, he's obsessed with serial killer Charles Manson. He claims that his 1969 copy of *LIFE* with Manson's picture on the cover is one of his most cherished possessions (*EW,* 11/19/93). Dando recorded the Manson tune, "Your Home is Where You're Happy" on his *Creator* album (1988). His rationale? "You might as well put Manson on the dollar bill. What's the difference? Who is George Washington anyway? Lincoln had slaves. American culture is built on rape and murder. What's the big deal about Charlie Manson?" (*Details,* 3/94).

Songs like "My Drug Buddy" and "Style" testify to his habitual drug use. And there are his nightmares and bouts of sleepwalking with his guitar. He's been known to wake the band up in the middle of the night, perched on the sink, screaming gibberish about things under the bed trying to kill him (*SPIN,* 4/93). His music seems to be the only thing that keeps him from going over the edge. "I've never met anyone like him," says drummer David Ryan. "I'll bet he's memorized about 10,000 songs. It's almost a form of autism. I think music is about all he has for dealing with his sadness. It's his salvation" (*EW,* 11/19/93). If that's true, it's a sad and shallow salvation. Jesus offers him so much more: "Peace I leave with you; My peace I give to you. I do not give to you as the world gives. So do not let your hearts be troubled, and do not be afraid" (Jn. 14:27; NIV, c.f., Jn. 16:33).

Music Exchange: Audio Adrenaline, Villanelle, the Waiting

Da LENCH MOB

This gansta-rap group literally lives the death and destruction they rap about. Two of the original trio were up on charges for murder. Lead rapper Dasean (J-Dee) Cooper was convicted of murder and sentenced to 29-years-to-life in prison for the crime. The murder occurred after Cooper got into an argument with a man at a party in 1993. According to witnesses, it all started when the man claimed Cooper's girlfriend was sleeping with other men. Cooper returned to the party with a gun and shot the man in the back as he fled. While awaiting trial, Cooper married another woman (*LAT,* 2/4/95).

Another member of the group, Terry (T-Bone) Gray, was accused of killing one person and wounding another in a bowling alley scuffle. The charges were dismissed as a case of mistaken identity (*AP Press,* 3/19/95). Since J-Dee is in jail, he's been replaced by Maulkie, a militant member of the Nation of Islam. In the tune, "Going Bananas," he raps: "*Oh my God! Allah have mercy / I'm killing these devils because they're not worthy / To walk the earth with the original Black Man / They must be forgettin' it's time for Armageddon*" (*The Source,* 1/95).

This rhetoric may sound fiercely powerful to the young impressionable fan, but it rings hollow in light of all the black-on-black violence. J-Dee shot a black man out of jealousy and selfishness, not for any noble motivations about the injustices of blacks throughout the world. The underlying qualities of this kind of rhetoric are arrogance and revenge—neither of which are spiritual qualities of the character of Christ (see Prov. 16:18, Isa. 10:33-34, 2 Sam. 22:28; and Lev. 19:18, Rom. 12:19, Nah. 1:2-3, Matt. 5:43-44).

There is no justification in the sight of God for the injustice done to blacks over the years. Nor is there justification in His sight for the violence they are perpetrating in the world today. We can debate these issues 'til the Kingdom comes, but the immediate question remains: what are you going to learn from these men and this music? "Do not associate with a man given to anger or go with a hot-tempered man, lest you learn his ways and find a snare for yourself" (Prov. 22:24-25, NAS).

Music Exchange: Apocalypse, Barry G., Gospel Ganstas, Grits, Preachas (P.I.D.), S.F.C., the S.S. M.O.B.

LIVE

These four friends from Yorktown, Pennsylvania were only 13 when they started their first band, Public Affection. Ten years later, LIVE (pronounced with a long -i-) became popular on the college radio circuits. The album *Throwing Copper* got lots of attention on MTV and went platinum in 1994. This alternative rock group is typical college-radio fare. The secular world sees them as bright and positive, and even a little mystical (i.e., spiritual). But from a Christian viewpoint, they are brooding doubters with a fascination for death. The song "Sh—Town" complains about growing up in a boring, small town. "Top" compares all religious leaders to Hitler (they seem to be just as disenchanted with New Age gurus as with phony televangelists). In "Selling the Drama" the singer opts to work out his salvation through his music instead of the Cross.

> "*All* we ever wanted to do was go on the road, do some drugs, play some rock, and have some sex."
> - Jennifer Finch of L7

The song "T.B.D." refers to the *Tibetan Book of the Dead*. "The song itself is about Aldus Huxley, who for the last 6 months of his life was taking LSD intravenously. During this time, his wife read to him from the Tibetan Book of the Dead, which describes how to spiritually and physically prepare yourself for death. Live thought it was a cool way to die and it inspired the song" (*Live's FAQ sheet,* 1/23/95). They may sound LIVE, but they won't do much for your Christian LIFE.

Music Exchange: Adam Again, Clash of Symbols, Dime Store Prophets, Grammatrain, Hocus Pick, LSU, Raspberry Jam

LOLLAPALOOZA. See PORNO FOR PYROS.

Courtney LOVE

Although Love leads her own grunge-punk band Hole, she's just as well known as The Great White Widow—wife of **Nirvana's** suicidal singer,

Kurt Cobain. Her father was a hippie who deserted the family to follow the **Grateful Dead** when she was five (1970). What followed was a whirlwind of communes, boarding schools, and foster homes. She was put in reform school at the age of 12 for shoplifting. Her social worker noted, "Love has a pattern of challenging adult authority, running away to avoid problems, and seeking immediate gratification of her needs. She repeatedly asks for authorities to find her a 'home.' Courtney is searching for the family life she has been deprived of for so many years" (*US*, 8/94). Still searching, Love was making a living in Japan as a stripper at the age of 14. At 16, she was the original singer for **Faith No More**. She also had a small role in the movie *Sid and Nancy* (the film about Sid Vicious of the **Sex Pistols**) while living in England.

She formed Hole in 1989 in Los Angeles and put out the album, *Pretty On the Inside* (1991), with its hit single "Teenage Whore." "Most of the songs are about bad sex, bad drugs, or a bad day at the abortion clinic. If this were a horror movie, it would be all the parts that you have to look at through your fingers" (*LAT*, 8/16/92). Hole is typical of the Riot Grrrl mentality: vulgar, angry, and loud. Love has been known to pull teenage boys up on stage, simulate sex with them, and then kick them back into the crowd (*VF*, 6/95). She often dives into the mosh pit, usually coming back to the stage with half her clothes ripped off (*CT*, 6/7/95). Her flair for the audacious is giving her the dubious distinction of being the first female rock superstar to hold her own in the male-dominated world of hard rock.

She married Kurt Cobain in 1992 and gave birth to their daughter, Frances Bean, later that year, amidst a flurry of controversy over whether she was doing heroin during her pregnancy (*VF*, 8/92). Cobain shot himself in April, 1994, as her second album was being released—the ironically titled *Live Through This*. More tragedy followed in June, when her bass player, Kristen Pfaff, was found dead in her apartment of a heroin overdose. Love claims to be coping with all this tragedy through Buddhism. She keeps Cobain's ashes in a shrine in her home. She studies *The Tibetan Book of the Dead.* "It has detailed descriptions of what happens when you die, and how you can help a dead person. That's really important to me: having control over the destiny of Kurt in terms of his spirit," she insists. She also regrets a period when her faith waned. "I'll tell you this right now, if I had not stopped chanting, Kurt would still be here—period, guaranteed, end of story" (*SPIN*, 2/95).

But Love's response to her personal tragedies has not been pretty inside. She went back to drugs after her husband's death, and an overdose of prescription drugs sent her to the hospital (*People*, 6/25/95). There have been bouts of angry acting out: an argument with a flight attendant, a fight with a male fan at a concert, punching out Kathleen Hannah of fellow-Riot Grrrls group Bikini Kill at Lollapalooza (*LAT*, 7/22/95). And there were her "too-soon" affairs with Trent Reznor of **Nine**

Inch Nails and Michael Stipe of **R.E.M.,** who talked her into exploring sex with other women (*VF,* 6/95). After all the years of searching, she still hasn't found a home or herself. God has a Way to make her feel at home, if only she'd stop looking for Love in all the wrong places.

Music Exchange: the Clergy, Morella's Forest, Ordained Fate, Plague of Ethyls

MADONNA

From the sacred to the sexual and from the proud to the profane, Madonna identifies and incriminates herself in her own words:

"Crucifixes are sexy, because there's a naked man on them" (*SPIN*, 6/85).

"Do you think I'm a pagan? I mean, I believe in the main God, the big one, and I believe in Jesus, but I believe in all the other ones too" (*IV*, 6/90).

"My show is not blasphemous. It's entertaining and educational. The moral is be strong, believe in freedom and in God, love yourself, understand your sexuality, have a sense of humor, masturbate, don't judge people by their religion, color, or sexual habits, love life and your family" (*FB*, 6/15/90). [*In that order?*]

On losing her virginity: "I thought it was a good career move" (*SH*, 12/85).

Q: Was your virginity something you wanted to get rid of?
A: "Definitely. It's a burden. I think all girls feel that way" (*Details*, 12/94).

"I don't think I'm using sex to sell myself" (*SL*, 1/87).

"Straight men need to be emasculated. I'm sorry, but they all need to be slapped around. Every straight guy should have a man's tongue in his mouth at least once" (*NW*, 5/27/91).

"I think your parents give you false expectations of life. All of us grow up completely misguided" (*SPIN*, 2/88).

"The actors and singers and entertainers I know are all emotional cripples. Let's face it, really healthy people aren't in this business" (*World*, 5/18/91).

"I know exactly what I want; if that makes me a bitch, okay!" (*SH*, 10/87).

"There's a modest side to me too" (*US*, 12/85). [Where?]

"I haven't overcome any big obstacles—all of my obstacles are still there. And ultimately, my big demons will always be there" (*SPIN*, 2/88).

Music Exchange: Lisa Bevill, Kim Boyce, Gina, Nicole, Tammy Trent

MARILYN MANSON

Marilyn Manson is not a girl. It is the name of a Florida-based goth-punk band and the name of the band's leader/singer. Like Manson (whose real name is Brian Warner), all of the band members have stage names composed of the first name of a female superstar and the last name of a male serial killer—Daisy Berkowitz, Twiggy Ramirez, Madonna Wayne Gacy, Sara Lee Lucas. It's a twisted attempt to say there is ugliness in the lives of the beautiful people and beauty in the mind of the mass murderer, and we all live somewhere in between (*RIP*, 2/95). Everything else about this band is equally as twisted. Their stage props include a shopping cart, live chickens, dice with all sixes, and a Lite-Brite that reads "Kill God." Their first album is called *Portrait of an American Family* (1994), which features such bizarre numbers as "Cake and Sodomy," "Dope Hat," and "Wrapped in Plastic." (Trent Reznor of **Nine Inch Nails** was so enthusiastic about these guys, he signed them to his *nothing* record label.) There is also an EP called *Smells Like Children* (such images have led to the rumor that Manson is a pedophile) and another album called *AntiChrist Superstar* (1996).

Manson use androgyny, the occult, and sensationalism in a misguided attempt to say something profound about the confusion and hypocrisy of American life. There are T-shirts with the red shield of the Salvation Army, inserting the words "The Satanic Army" instead. They also sell a T-shirt that says, "Kill God...Kill Your Mom and Dad...Kill Yourself." They were banned in Salt Lake City while on the *Self-Destruct* tour with Nine Inch Nails because of such material. Manson and Reznor protested together on stage by tearing up a Bible (*LAT,* 10/5/94).

Unlike **White Zombie,** Marilyn Manson's occultism is not a comic book Satanism simply calculated to perturb parents. They claim to have "a special place" in Anton Lavey's organization (the Satanic Church of America), because of their power to sway today's youth. Manson understands the more insidious side of Satanism. "I go by the attitude 'do what you will' that is the whole of the law. [This is a direct reference to the supreme principle of the infamous occultist, Aleister Crowley.] And I will do exactly that. Satanism is not about a devil. It's about realizing, much like Nietzsche said, that you are your own god. I guess a word for it is 'me-ism,' because it's a very selfish philosophy" (*RIP,* 2/95).

This is not a band that you can excuse with "I just like their music." "I'm here to call Christian America on their bluff," he says (*Faces,* 2/95). "Christianity is just another product, so you figure out which lie works best for you. That's all they are—they're all lies. Even if there is a God, that doesn't mean you have to worship it. I believe in myself" (*RIP,* 10/95).

"The message that I'm sending out to America is 'raise your kids better or I'll be raising them for you.' I want to raise kids in truth and tell them that everything is a lie—there is no truth!" (*RIP,* 2/95). [Is that really true, Marilyn? Are you sure you aren't lying to us? How can we be sure?] Marilyn says the truth is a lie. God says the Truth will set you free (John 8:38). There is no middle ground here. As **Amy Grant** sings, you have to decide "who to and who not to listen to."

Music Exchange: Fell Venus

BOB MARLEY
• •
Born in a poor section of Jamaica, Bob Marley eventually gained worldwide popularity through his music. He was originally introduced to Kingston record producers by Jimmy Cliff in 1962. A year later he formed The Wailers with Peter Tosh and Bunny Wailer. When the group turned to Rastafari as their religion, they forged a permanent link between reggae and Rasta. [see Reggae Music on page XXX.] By the mid-'70s, Marley was touring Europe with Johnny Nash and **Eric Clapton,** who had recorded hit versions of his music.

Despite his international popularity, Marley saw little of the money. His political opinions and campaign to legalize marijuana made him unpopular with the establishment. An assassination attempt in 1976 is generally credited to his political enemies. He died of brain cancer in 1981, leaving behind eleven children fathered through seven different women and a multimillion dollar estate that is in total disarray. He is considered a martyred hero by many Jamaicans and is a prophet in the minds of many Rastas. Some believe that the spirit of Bob Marley resides in all true reggae singers, or that his son Ziggy Marley is his reincarnation. Although he died over a decade ago, Bob Marley remains the most popular reggae artist in the world today.

Reggae music is generally a light, listenable style. Bouncy tunes about Jah love and peace may deceive listeners into thinking this is a Christian message, but Rasta is *not* Christianity. And there are those who use reggae/rasta's "spiritualizing" of "de 'erb" (also called de ganja) as an excuse to get high on marijuana. Curiosity about Rasta could open the door to a wise and guided study of comparative religions. Or it can lead to the deception of rationalizing offbeat behaviors and beliefs as being Christian.

Music Exchange: Children of Israel, Christafari, Ben Okafor, Reggae Worship

METALLICA

Once an extreme example of the unknown underground of speed metal,

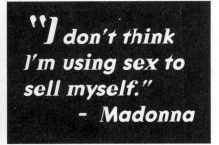

"*I don't think I'm using sex to sell myself.*"
— Madonna

Metallica managed to move thrash metal into the mainstream and onto the top of the charts. Metallica is almost two distinctly different bands. The first phase started in 1981 in Los Angeles when Danish-born Lars Uhlrich met James Hetfield and Dave Mustaine. Anxious to put the "heavy" back into heavy metal, they left for San Francisco to finds fans who were not posing as the kings (or queens) of L.A.'s glitzy glam-metal scene.

Mustaine left the band to form Megadeth and was replaced by Kirk Hammet (from Exodus) before the group recorded their first album. Early albums—*Kill 'Em All* (1983), *Ride The Lightning* (1984), and *Master of Puppets* (1986)—can best be described as 67 ways to die. Songs like "Creeping Death" and "Trapped Under the Ice" were sinister serenades to dying slowly. Bassist Cliff Burton died in a bus accident while touring Sweden in 1986, and was replaced by Jason Newsted (of Flotsam & Jetsam), and the band played on.

Phase Two started with the release of their social/political concept album *...And Justice For All* (1988). They once swore they would never do a video for MTV, but they broke that promise on this album. And the

90

video for the song "One" sent the group's popularity and sales through the roof. Almost entirely abandoning their speed-metal style, the follow-up album, *Metallica* (1991), reflected the mellow sounds of "One" and actually included several ballads. While the older fans were crying "sell-out," newer, younger fans were buying it, until it sold over 10 million copies worldwide. A massive compilation package, *Binge and Purge*, included three CDs, three videos, concert memorabilia, and a $75 price tag, which scared off everyone except the most devoted fans.

Most metal bands are fairly obvious, crude, and unsophisticated. This isn't entirely the case with Metallica, and it makes for a more challenging analysis. The early albums put the band at the head of the death and dismemberment pack, which later spawned the breeds of metal known as Death Metal and Grindcore (see the Introduction for definitions of these terms). In those days, Ulrich's alcoholic excesses were well known, and the band took a typical "metal-may-care" attitude toward groupies and drugs. The later albums offer a much moodier view of life and death in America.

The band's main lyrical theme is death, and they cover every aspect of the subject, from the dramatic and cruel, to the subtle and sophisticated. Hetfield is perhaps the best writer of this genre and his terse poetry evokes a variety of emotions and images in very few words. The tune "Fade to Black" is an insightful, yet irresponsible, rationale for teen suicide. "Dyers Eve" is another suicide song, but this one blames cruel, repressive parents for the deed. The video for "One" used footage from an anti-war film called *Johnny Get Your Gun* (1971) to drive home the song's depressing cry for death.

Fans of the newer Metallica justify listening to the band by pointing out that they've softened quite a bit lately. Their music isn't as hard as it used to be and they no longer sing about brutally satanic themes. While all that's true, they still must grapple with Metallica's nihilistic and hopeless portrait of life. This constant focus on death instead of life is not healthy for the spirit. And for all their poetic insight, there are very few solutions here. As always, we must look to the Lord to find the perfect balance of mercy and justice for all.

Music Exchange: Believer, early Deliverance, Detritus, Jesus Freaks, Tourniquet

MINISTRY

This industrial music project is primarily the brainchild of Alain Jourgensen. Born in Cuba, his family moved to Denver after the Communist revolution in the 1950s. Unable to get along with his folks, he dropped out of high school and worked himself through college (he claims to be one semester short of a degree in history—*LAT*, 8/2/92). Inspired by the pre-punk antics of the Ramones, Jourgensen formed Ministry in 1981. His first effort was the surprisingly insipid album "With Sympathy" (1983)—a synthesized new wave dance effort remarkably similar to **Depeche Mode.**

Settling in the Chicago area, Jourgensen worked as a sales clerk at a record store called Wax Trax. The store evolved into an independent record company, and Jourgensen became a prolific record producer, with projects like Blackout, Pale Head, 1,000 Homo DJ's, Lard (with Jello Biafra of the **Dead Kennedys**), and Acid Horse (with the Cabaret Voltaire). He has also produced a couple of albums with his sarcastic side-project, The Revolting Cocks, also known as RevCo—*Beers, Steers, & Queers* (1990) and 1993's *Linger Ficken' Good and Other Barnyard Oddities* (with LSD guru Timothy Leary ranting about empowerment on a tune called "Gila Copter").

But it is his serious side in Ministry that has gotten him the most attention. Although most people consider Jourgensen the godfather of the American industrial music scene, he prefers to call his music *aggro-rock* to describe his style (an *aggregate* or fusion of styles like house music, thrash metal, punk, disco funk, and even country) and his attitude and approach to his music—*aggressive aggravation.*

Albums like *Twitch* (1986), *Land of Rape and Honey* (1988), and *A Mind is a Terrible Thing To Taste* (1989) grew increasingly harder and more abrasive as he expressed his terror-inducing vision of the great American apocalypse. The intense visual impact of his music comes across on the live concert video *In Case You Didn't Feel Like Showing Up* (1991). The chaotic collage of sounds coming from these projects often seems to be the product of a demented mind, and it's not surprising to discover that these albums were fueled by Jourgensen's heavy use of heroin, LSD, and Jack Daniels whiskey (*RS*, 4/18/91). Jourgensen was eventually arrested near his home in Austin, Texas for possession of heroin, marijuana, and drug paraphernalia in August, 1995. The band's guitarist, Mike Scaccia, was also arrested for heroin possession at a local Wal-Mart the very same day (*RS*, 10/19/95).

Ministry remained a fixture in the industrial underground until the album *Psalm 69* (1992). "The album is named after a chapter of noted occult mystic Aleister Crowley's book *The Book of Lies*, which translates as *Psalm 69: The Way to Succeed and the Way to Suck Eggs*—Crowley's disturbed reference to oral sex" (*AP*, 10/92). The album featured a hit single called "Jesus Built My Hotrod" which mocks the concept of faith in Christ; and the title tune "Psalm 69," which distorts some evangelist's cries of "hallelujah" until it sounds like someone screaming "Heil, Hitler!" "Organized religion is just a big piece of sh** that basically preys on people's fears. It's just like a big insurance scam. Keep them frightened, and they'll do what you say" (*RIP*, 4/93).

Ministry's popularity also began to soar when they toured with the second Lollapalooza festival in the summer of 1992. Dressed like some kind of cowboy-biker from hell, Jourgensen performed his demented diatribes behind "a mic stand covered in animal bones crowned with a Satanic-looking goat's skull" (*RIP*, 8/95). It's a reflection of Jourgensen's morbid hobby of collecting dead things. "I have 1,100 skulls," he boasts, "Steers, dogs, cats, havalinas. Notice the pig fetus, right next to the rat? Hey, they were already dead—roadkill and stuff—we didn't *kill* them. I just like it, aesthetically" (*RIP*, 10/94). Ministry's album *Filth Pig* (1995) continues in the same doom and death dimensions, only slower and darker.

Jourgensen says his anger is about his fear for the future of his daughter, Adrian. It's aimed at the sedentary selfishness of right-wing America, that mindless glob of humanity mesmerized by the media, whose only interest seems to be to collect more electronic gadgets for their own comfort (*RIP*, 4/93). It's an ironic perspective in light of his well-publicized dream of owning his own recording studio with all the latest electronic gadgets, which he now has in his new home near Austin, Texas.

Despite this fiercely opinionated posturing, he confesses that he has no answers to the problems he points out with such righteous indignation. He just wants to whip the

> "**T**he message that I'm sending out to America is 'raise your kids better or I'll be raising them for you.' I want to raise kids in truth and tell them that everything is a lie—there is no truth!"
> - **Marilyn Manson**

world into a frenzy of angry chaos, thinking that will bring us closer to solutions for our lives. Perhaps he's never noticed that stirring up a hornet's nest does not make those insects more productive. They just sting anyone who happens to be disturbing their nest. Appealing as this portrait might be to some of his fans, this kind of Ministry won't heal America or the Christian soul.

Music Exchange: Argyle Park, Chatterbox, Brainchild/Circle of Dust, Deitiphobia, Electro Shock Therapy, Fell Venus, Generation, Global Wave System, Mortal, Under Midnight, X-Propagation

MOBY

Moby is a study in extremes. Born Richard Melville Hall in 1965, he was nicknamed Moby after distant relative Herman Melville's novel, *Moby Dick*. After his father died in an auto accident, he went back and forth between his grandparents' country club lifestyle and his pot-smoking hippie mom's apartment. During his teen years, Moby swung from the heavy metal stoner lifestyle to the anti-drug stance of straight-edged punk (with his own punk band, Vatican Commando). In college, he was an alcoholic party-animal, until he became a passionate Christian and a militant vegetarian. As a dance club DJ, he had penchant for mixing the country sounds of Hank Williams, Sr. with the industrial noise of Throbbing Gristle. These days, the often-bald techno-rave artist produces dance music from his apartment in New York City.

Moby started recording his own music between 1989 and 1992 in a series of singles for Instinct Records, which were later collected and released as albums: *Moby* (1992), *Early Underground* (1993) and *Ambient* (1993). His first big hit was "Go," a variation on the weird theme music of *Twin Peaks*. He also produced a novelty dance tune called "Thousand," which at 1,000 bpm may be the fastest song ever recorded. His EP, *Move* (1993) was followed by the LP *Everything Is Wrong* (1995), which was described as "a melee of conflicting emotions and musical styles," (*RS,* 5/4/95) and "a tossed salad of emotions that stands in contrast to the iceberg lettuce of his peers" (*OPT,* 5-6/95). Musically it's an eclectic mix of punk, reggae, gospel, and disco, including an inspiring eight-minute classical instrumental called "God Moving Over The Face of the Waters." It's as if Moby is determined to express every extreme of his experience and his emotions in one liquid whole. "The music I make is sad and joyful, tragic and happy. Life is about laughing and crying and singing and screaming, all at the same time" (*Details,* 4/95).

Moby, like his music, is a collage of conflicting concepts. He is decidedly passionate about his Christianity, an unpopular position in hedonistic rave circles. Like many of his fans, he is disenchanted with the church, and prefers to find God in people and life at large: "Just look at how intensely complicated the fabric of existence is. I think that indicates the majesty of God" (*Details,* 4/95). His grasp of Christ seems pretty clear "Christ wasn't complacent. If He had been complacent, he wouldn't have gotten nailed to that tree" (*OPT,* 5-6/95). But his theology can be pretty muddy. He says that dance music is really about salvation, and he thinks that Christ's crucifixion was a type of suicide, justifying the suicide of Kurt Cobain (of **Nirvana**) and others. Working with the militant animal activists PETA (People for the Ethical Treatment of Animals), he often sports a T-shirt that declares: Jesus was a vegetarian [apparently

94

fish doesn't count] (*AP*, 11/95). He is also pro-choice on the abortion issue and sexually active, although not married.

While artistic intellectuals often make unconventional Christians, Moby wanders pretty far afield. As a lone ranger Christian, he seems to be making the classic mistake of being too smart for his own good. He doesn't appear to be under any spiritual accountability or discipleship in his life. He needs to learn to rationalize a little less and believe a little more. He apparently understands Christ as Savior, but not as Lord. And even he seems to realize that there's something mixed-up in his Christian mix: "I don't know that heaven will *look* like anything. It would just *be* everything—pure understanding. And people wouldn't have to hide. I don't know if I'll end up there, you know—too much anal sex" (*Details*, 4/95).

Music Exchange: Scott Blackwell, Prodigal Sons, Raving Loonatics

MORBID ANGEL
••

This Florida quartet originally formed in 1984, led by self-styled occultist David Vincent, the singer and spokesman. Guitarist Trey Azagthoth, named himself after the Sumerian god of war and disorder and claims to be a demon and a vampire. He gained instant infamy for the band at the New Music Seminar in 1990 by biting himself and drinking his own blood during their performance (*SPIN*, 6/91). Occult themes abound in albums like *Altars of Madness* (1989) and *Blessed Are The Sick* (1991) (with lyrics like: "*World of sickness / Blessed are we / To taste this life of Sin*"). Their hatred of Christianity rages in tunes like "Unholy Blasphemies" ("*Ghouls who pray the death of God / Destroy Jehovah's Church / Vomit upon the Cross / And burn the Book of lies*"). *Covenant* (1993) features more of the same, only it's distributed by a major label (Giant) and is unfortunately much easier to find.

Few bands capture the meaning of death metal better than Morbid Angel. Their screeching guitars and sinister vocals are a sales pitch for a holiday in Hell. However, unlike **King Diamond** or **Deicide**, they are not strictly Satanists. They dabble in a variety of viewpoints to concoct their own brand of darkness. "Are they satanic? Absolutely, but according to their own definition. It's got more to do with a devastated world view, wrapped in philosophical armor culled from Nietzsche, Eastern thought, horror flicks, paganism, Anton Lavey, and Aleister Crowley—whose tenet, 'Do What Thou Wilt' is the key to understanding Vincent's personal left-hand path. He's a spiritual libertarian" (*RIP*, 9/93).

"Satanism isn't really the word for what we're about. Evil, perhaps, but we do much more than just sing about the devil. This idea of actually worshipping the Devil, like the idea of worshipping Christ—I don't find it to be very intelligent. It's still having a master over the self. Satanism could very easily be *self*-ism or humanism," explains Vincent (*Hard and Heavy* video interview, 1992).

Morbid Angel's self-mastery is a myth. When they sing "Immortal Rites" (*"Lord of death, I summon you / Reside within our brains / Cast your spells upon our lives / So that we may receive / The gift of immortality / Bestowed on those who seek you"*), they're giving their lives to a cruel master. They are playing with fire—and so are the fans who follow them. Just because they don't see Satan, doesn't mean he isn't there. A demon by any other name can still send you to Hell.

Music Exchange: Living Sacrifice, Mortification, Tourniquet, Vengeance Rising

Alanis MORISSETTE

Although relatively new to the American music scene, Canadian singer/songwriter Alanis Morissette has been in the entertainment business most of her life. Born and raised in Ottawa, she recorded her first single at the age of 10 and was signed to MCA Records at 14. By her mid-teens, she was known simply by her first name—kind of a Canadian Tiffany producing pop/dance albums like *Alanis* (1990) and *Now Is The Time* (1992). She was also a semi-regular on Nickelodeon's "You Can't Do That On TV." But the pressures of popularity and the pace of living in the media fast lane took its toll. Morissette missed her childhood and grew up too fast.

At the age of 20, Morissette signed on with **Madonna's** record label, Maverick, and came roaring back with a bitter little album called *Jagged Little Pill* (1995). Filled with anguished outrage, the album lashes out at every boyfriend and businessman that ever betrayed or abused her. For instance, her hit song "You Oughta Know" has her walking up to an ex-boyfriend at his wedding reception, screaming vindictively: *"Did you forget about me, Mr. Duplicity? / I hate to bug you in the middle of dinner / It was a slap in the face how quickly I was replaced / Are you thinking of me when you f*** her?"* On "Right Through You" she confronts a manipulative music exec with *"You took me for a child / You took a long hard look at my ass / You took me out to wine, dine, and 69 me / But you didn't hear a damn word I said."* Despite the abrasive mood and explicit language, the album got lots of airplay on modern rock stations, because musically, it's edgier than **Melissa Etheridge,** but not as abrasive as **Liz Phair** or **Courtney Love.**

Morissette excuses her explicit rage as an honest emotional release. "I never meant to hurt anybody. It's more of an honesty thing for me. I write for the sake of release" (*BAM*, 8/11/95). After her exposure to the selfish hypocrisy of the music business at too young and vulnerable an age, she probably does need to get in touch with her anger. But this work is best done in professional therapy or with trusted friends, not on a record sold to teens. Even though many of her young listeners might relate to feelings of betrayal, how many young Christian girls are going to express it like this? And when did anger become the last honest emotion left to humanity? Being happy isn't considered honest, it's simply naive. Expressing Christian faith isn't honest, it's called hypocritical. According to the media, the only true emotion left to humanity is anger. And that's a rather narrow-minded and one-dimensional perspective of people, don't you think?

Music Exchange: Dakota Motor Company, Nina, Raspberry Jam, Riki Michelle

Van MORRISON

Born in Ireland in 1945, this classic folk-rocker has put out nearly 30 albums in his career. He formed the band Them in 1964 and had some hits like "Here Comes the Night" and "Gloria." Morrison went solo and had several Top 40 hits of his own, like "Brown-Eyed Girl" (1967) and "Domino" (1970). As he continued to put out albums, his music took on a more spiritual, meditative quality. He won a Grammy in 1988 for *Irish Heartbeat,* a traditional Irish folk album performed with the Chieftains. He remains musically active in the 1990s with albums like *Enlightenment* and *Hymns To the Silence.* Morrison is constantly compared to Dylan as a lyrical prophet, and such artists as **Bruce Springsteen,** Bob Seeger, and **U2** tout him as a major inspiration in their music.

Many Christians are drawn to Morrison's inspiring and spiritual music. Songs like "His Master's Eyes" (from *Sense of Wonder,* 1985) and "Whenever God Shines His Light" (with Cliff Richards, from *Avalon Sunset,* 1989) reflect an honest search for God and a genuine gratefulness for His gifts. However, his understanding of Christianity seems to be a bit muddy. For example, he claims to have been a Christian all his life: "It's something I've always carried. There was no conversion experience. Not at all. I'd say I'm a Christian. I've been a Christian since I was born" (*Musician,* 6/83).

It's no wonder, considering how eclectic his spiritual influences have been. Morrison was raised a Jehovah's Witness. He was briefly involved with Scientology and thanks L. Ron Hubbard on the album *Inarticulate Speech of the Heart.* He tried TM (transcendental meditation) only to discover that he'd actually been doing it all his life (*Musician,* 4/87). His record company bio cites such diverse influences as Alice Bailey (New Age channeler), Krishnamurti (Hindu mystic), and the teachings of the Christian mystics.

Is Morrison a confused Christian creating his own answers from a spiritual smorgasbord? Or is he a sensitive searcher sifting for answers in the religious marketplace? He is an artist that deserves some deep discussion, especially with bright young adult "seekers." In truth, he offers a unique and artistic picture of faith that will challenge any thoughtful Christian.

Music Exchange: Eden Burning, Nicholas Giaconia, Mark Heard, Derek Lind, Mike Roe (of the 77's), Randy Stonehill

NAPALM DEATH

"Napalm Death is widely recognized as having pioneered the musical genre known as grindcore—a lethal mixture of death metal and hardcore played at extreme, dazzling speeds" (*MM*, 10/90). Starting out in Birmingham, England in the mid-1980s, they became known as the fastest band in the world (a claim constantly being challenged by newer, younger bands). They offer such complex musical masterpieces as "The Kill" (all of 12 seconds long) and "You Suffer (But Why?)" which came in at 3 seconds. Albums like *Scum* (1987), *From Enslavement to Obliteration* (1988), and *Mentally Murdered* (1989) put this group deeply in the "death and dismemberment" club. As fathers of the genre, they have begotten several ill-bred descendants. The original drummer left to form **Godflesh**, and one of the guitarists left to form Carcass.

The band's name speaks volumes as they pour out their anger in descriptions of the gory destruction of everything they think they hate, including music itself. The ads for *Utopia Banished* (1992) claimed it was "a campaign for musical destruction." They refer to themselves as "The End of Music As We Know It." Put quite simply, "This is ugly music made by outcasts with no interest in conforming to any standards" (*RIP*, 3/93). Most parents would certainly agree. Any Christian who can't (or won't) see this music as unhealthy for the spirit is definitely struggling with his faith and joy (Col. 2:8).

Music Exchange: Detritus, Living Sacrifice, Mortification, Seventh Angel, Vengeance Rising

NAUGHTY BY NATURE

This New Jersey hip-hop trio temporarily took the focus off the L.A. scene (N.W.A., Ice Cube, Ice-T) and brought it back to the East Coast, where rap got its start. Queen Latifah helped out on the first album, *Naughty By Nature* (1991), but it was the infectious tune, "(Are You Down With) O.P.P." that got all the attention. The initials stand for "Other People's Property" (or "Other People's Private Parts") and it urged listeners to ignore their current partners and simply give in to any sexual impulse that comes along. "The video brought out their roughneck 'wild in the penile' image—complete with braids, baggy pants, menacing scowls, and (lead rapper) Treach's machete" (*The Source*, 1/92). The follow-up albums, *19 Naughty III* (1993) and *Poverty Paradise* (1995), focus more on the social ills of the 'hood, but they are still not spiritually healthy. The relatively inoffensive rap rallying cry of "Hip Hop Hooray" can't justify the other tunes filled with misogyny, multiple partners, and oral sex. We are already naughty by nature (Rom. 3:23), we don't need these guys' help to get down with it.

Music Exchange: Dynamic Twins, Barry G., Grits, S.F.C., T-Bone

NINE INCH NAILS

Actually, NIN is the work of one man, Trent Reznor, who was raised in rural Pennsylvania and brought up by his religious grandparents in Cleveland after his parents divorced. His first album, *Pretty Hate Machine* (1989), brought industrial music to the masses with its anguished, but accessible, dance tunes. The album went largely unnoticed until it was given extensive exposure when Reznor performed at the first Lollapalooza Festival in 1991. Reznor is a tortured soul, and he sounds fierce but frightened as he screams lyrics like: *"Head like a hole / black as your soul / I'd rather die / Than give you control!"* The music, with its driving beats and fist-in-your-face lyrics, is basically punk music set to a synthesizer.

The album *Downward Spiral* (1994) is an agonizing descent into anger and despair. The video for his hit single "Closer" is washed in bleak browns, and the stark, deadly imagery is reminiscent of those World War II-era films showing the devastation of the concentration camps. To add to the eerie ambiance, Reznor wrote and recorded the album in the house where Sharon Tate was murdered by members of the Manson Family. He expresses his fear of being controlled in songs like "Mr. Self-Destruct" and "March of the Pigs." He resists religious trappings on "Heresy," and wonders about the power of suicide on the title track.

Reznor says he does it to help people feel better. Feeling alienated and without a friend as a kid, he went home after school to listen to Pink Floyd and the **Cure**. "It made me feel almost normal, hearing someone who was more depressed than me." If that's true, his fans must be feeling better, because there's nothing more depressing than these albums.

Most alternative music reflects the despair of nihilism with a "poor me, I'm a loser, and everything sucks" attitude. Reznor (and other industrial artists like **Ministry** and **Skinny Puppy**) virtually howl with rage. But it doesn't come pouring out of them in uncontrolled mania. It is searched for, deliberated on, massaged, and savored. Despite Reznor's rationalizations to the contrary, this deliberate descent into the dark side profits no one. It doesn't ease anyone's conscience or soothe anyone's guilt. It fans the flames of hatred and hysterics that lead to true self-destruction. Reznor worries about the addictions that can control us, never admitting that his own fierce focus is an addiction of its own. Anger's fire is a parable of Hell on earth. It burns without consuming, out of control; it is destructive beyond measure. The only way out is to walk away from it and embrace the peace that passes understanding.

Music Exchange: Argyle Park, Chatterbox, Brainchild/Circle of Dust, Deitiphobia, Electro Shock Therapy, Fell Venus, Generation, Global Wave System, Mortal, Under Midnight, X-Propagation

NIRVANA

This Seattle trio brought grunge rock to the nation and became the spokesmen for the jaded alienation of Generation X. The tragic life of the band's leader, Kurt Cobain, began with his parents' divorce when he was seven. He was shuffled from home to home, until he headed for Seattle on his own. He met Chris Novoselic at art school, and they started playing punk clubs in the area. Their first album was called *Bleach* (1989), recorded on Seattle's independent grunge label Sub Pop. Nirvana's major label debut, *Nevermind* (1991), was a multi-platinum sensation. Everything about it was controversial and (therefore) appealing to the next-big-thing crowd. The album cover featured a naked baby boy swimming for a dollar. The songs were muddy and indistinct, but "Smells Like Teen Spirit" (a reference to a brand of underarm deoderant marketed to teens) was a huge hit single. "Lithium" compared religion to the mind-numbing drug. "People who are secluded too long go insane, and as a last resort they often use religion to keep alive," explained Cobain on their record company bio. "In the song, a guy's lost his girl and he's brooding. He decides to find God before he kills himself. It's hard to understand the need for a vice like that, but I can appreciate it. People need vices."

Cobain's success supported a debilitating heroin habit, which he shared with **Courtney Love**, whom he married in 1992. Controversy erupted over rumors that Love was doing heroin while pregnant with their daughter, Frances Bean (*VF*, 8/92). *Incesticide* (1992), an album full of rejected B-sides, was released to grunge-hungry fans while Cobain tried to get his act together and get a real album out. That album was *In Utero* (1993), and it was filled with the same tortured angst that fueled the band's original success. In March of 1994, Cobain was hospitalized in Rome, comatose after overdosing on champaign and tranquilizers. A month later, on April 8, he was found dead in his home, from a self-inflicted shotgun wound.

His suicide generated more rock music press and commentary than anything since John Lennon's death in 1980. Some mourned him as a martyr, some dismissed him as a loser, some followed him in suicidal sympathy. Everyone recognized how well he reflected the feelings of the new rock generation. But relating isn't healing, and neither Nirvana nor Cobain had an answer to this generation's perceived pain. His suicide only served to dismantle the myth that the fame and money of a rock star will make you happy. Ultimately, there was nothing noble about the way Cobain lived or died. That's not entirely his fault. He needed someone to help him make the transition from Nirvana to Heaven.

Music Exchange: Applehead, Clash of Symbols, Grammatrain, Sometime Sunday, Wish For Eden, Yonderboy

The Notorious B.I.G.

Also known as Biggie Smalls, Chris Wallace is an aptly named rapper at 6'3" and 280 lbs. He dropped out of school in the 11th grade and cruised his New York neighborhood selling crack cocaine. At 17, he spent nine months in a North Carolina jail for drug dealing. In the summer of 1995, he was arrested for assaulting a man and stealing his portable phone and jewelry (*USA Today*, 6/19/95). His debut album *Ready To Die* (1994) is "a collection of gripping tales of violence, pain, and desperation" (*L.A. Times*, 3/27/95). It is a dark portrayal of his experience on the streets, and includes songs about drugs, sexual fantasies with famous females, and an unsettling tune called "Suicidal Thoughts." While he seems to rap about what he knows, what he knows is only the darkest side of life. While that may be real for him, it really only offers no solution to the kids who listen to him. Our kids need to hear more about how to find true Life, and less about looking at life on a dead-end street. "Do not associate with a man given to anger or go with a hot-tempered man, lest you learn his ways and find a snare for yourself" (Prov. 22:24-25, NAS).

Music Exchange: Dynamic Twins, Gospel Ganstas, Grits, Preachas, S.F.C., King Shon & the S.S. M.O.B., T-Bone

N.W.A.

This Los Angeles-area rap crew has the distinction of being the first popular gansta rap group. The initials stand for Niggaz Wit(h) Attitude, and they have done their best to live up to the name. Their first national release, *Straight Outta Compton* (1989), sold over 2 million copies and featured the violently controversial cut "F*** the Police" with its rebellious call to kill cops: *"Punk police are afraid of me / A young nigger on the warpath / And when I finish, it's gonna be a bloodbath / Of cops dying in L.A."* "The stark, brutal depictions of gang life and urban warfare; the coarse, obscene language, and the completely amoral tone (of the album), earned N.W.A. scorn from middle-class types of all colors and attempts from the FBI to keep retailers from stocking it" (*AMG*, pg. 649).

Their follow-up, *Niggaz4Life* (1991), became the first hardcore gansta rap album to hit #1 on the Billboard charts, although there was not one cut on the album fit to be played on radio. It contains 223 uses of the "F" word, "nigga" (205), "bitch" (84), and over 150 other obscene words (*NMR*, 6/14/91). In addition to the language and the glorified violence, the album added demeaning attitudes toward women to its catalogue of crimes with raps like "One Less Bitch," "To Kill A Hooker," and "Find 'em, F*** 'em, and Flee." "*Niggaz4Life* is a rap mural of ghetto life, spray-painted with blood" (*Time*, 7/1/91).

Claiming to offer realistic portraits of ghetto life, N.W.A. consistently refused to take responsibility for glorifying gang violence and contributing to the problem. Rap fans say the music is simply about real life, but they cannot explain how any of this music makes real life better. In the world of rap music, you can justify just about anything, if you rap it up in the right package.

Music Exchange: Dynamic Twins, E.T.W., Gospel Ganstas, S.F.C., King Shon & the S.S. M.O.B.

N.W.A. began to disintegrate in 1990 when Ice Cube left for a solo career. Eazy-E officially disbanded the crew in 1992. Since then, there have been constant verbal battles, suits, and brawls among band members. N.W.A. had a number of lesser-known members, including M.C. Ren, D.J. Yella, the Arabian Prince, and the D.O.C., but the key members went on to have notable solo careers. They include:

EAZY-E. A former gang member and drug dealer from Compton, Eric "Eazy-E" Wright started N.W.A. and Ruthless Records in 1986 to get his rap down. His first solo effort, *Eazy-Duz-It* (1988), was even more obnoxious and obscene than N.W.A.'s *Straight Outta Compton* (1989). Wright kept himself in the news with constant, if somewhat unexpected, controversy. In 1991, he began attending political luncheons and rallies in support of President Bush. At the invitation of Arnold Schwarzennegger, he payed $2,500 in dues to join the Republican Senatorial Inner Circle. Despite his reputation as being militantly anti-police, he made the headlines again in 1993 when he came out in support of one of the police officers being tried in the infamous Rodney King incident.

Blatantly outspoken, Eazy-E was in constant verbal and court battles with ex-members of N.W.A., **Ice Cube**, and **Dr. Dre**. Ice Cube called him a sell-out in his album *Death Certificate* (1991), and Dr. Dre dissed (disrespected) him on *The Chronic* (1993), mocking him with a wimpy lookalike in the video for "Dre Day." Eazy-E shot back on the album *It's On (Dr. Dre 187UM) Killa* (1993). Despite all the bickering, Eazy-E was a successful businessman and record producer.

Ultimately, however, his lifestyle caught up with him. In March, 1995, Eazy-E announced that he had tested positive for AIDS. In a public statement, he attributed the disease to his promiscuous lifestyle of unprotected sex, claiming that he had sex with hundreds of female fans, fathering seven children by six different women (*SPIN*, 5/95). He died ten days later on March 26, 1995.

Music Exchange: Disciples of Christ, Michael Peace, T-Bone,

ICE CUBE. O'Shea "Ice Cube" Jackson was the first to leave N.W.A. in 1990 over finances. He claimed their manager, Jerry Heller, was taking most of the group's profits for himself. His first album, *AmeriKKKa's Most Wanted* (1990), established him as one of the most graphic gangsta rapper's in the 'hood. His subsequent portrayal as a gang member in John Hughe's movie *Boyz 'n the Hood* (1991) solidified his reputation. The stark, violent images of the rage and turmoil of the inner city in *Death Certificate* (1991) was an almost prophetic portrayal of the L.A. riots which occurred months after it's release. The album also highlighted a racist attitude which advocated killing Koreans and Jewish record company types (like Jerry Heller). *Kill at Will* (1991), *The Predator* (1992), and *Lethal Injection* (1993) continued in the same vein. It's been suggested that Ice Cube's commitment to Islam and his family (he is married with two children) have softened his edge, but that remains to be seen.
Music Exchange: Preachas, S.F.C., King Shon & the S.S. M.O.B.

DR. DRE. Andre "Dr. Dre" Young rose from the ranks of N.W.A. to become one of the most powerful men in rap music today. He started out with the World Class Wreckin' Cru in 1985. He left to join Eazy-E, Ice Cube, and M.C. Ren to form N.W.A. in 1988. Like former crew-mate Ice Cube, he left N.W.A. in a dispute over getting his share of the finances. He started his own label, Death Row Records, which has become one of the predominant forces in rap production, with acts like Snoop Doggy Dogg, Warren G., **Mary J. Blige**, and **Jodeci.** In 1993, his album, *The Chronic* (street slang for a potent type of pot), became one of the top ten albums of the year. It bears the legend, "In Bud We Trust" and the CD sports a picture of a marijuana leaf. "The $20 Sack Pyramid" offers a detailed "how to" for drug deals and advocates open drug use on the streets (*LAT,* 2/14/93).

While his public life has been quite successful, the same can't be said for his private life. In 1991, he was sued for $23 million by Dee Barnes for assault and battery. Barnes was the VJ for a rap video show called "Pump It Up." Dre was reportedly upset because she aired an interview with Ice Cube that criticized members of N.W.A. "I just did it, you know," he admitted. "Besides, it ain't no big thing—I just threw her through a door" (*LAT,* 7/23/91). (In subsequent interviews, Eazy-E claimed "The bitch deserved it" and M.C. Ren said he "hoped it happened again" (*BB,* 1/25/92). The pattern continued in 1992 with an assault on a record producer (Dre broke his jaw in a fight), and a brawl with New Orleans police. In 1994, he was sentenced to five months in jail for a drunk-driving incident which violated his parole for the previous incidents. As Forrest Gump might say, "Brutal is as brutal does." "Do not be envious of evil men, nor desire to be with them, for their minds devise violence, and their lips talk of trouble" (Prov. 24:1-2).

Music Exchange: Barry G., Gospel Ganstas, King Shon & the S.S. M.O.B.

OFFSPRING

Offspring is part of the punk/hardcore revival in America that started in the early '90s (along with **Green Day**). At first, they don't seem to be typical punks. They aren't a bunch of antisocial dropouts. They are over 30. One has a college degree in finance, another in electronics, and the singer is working on a Ph.D. in molecular biology. Nor are they an underground phenomenon. Their third album, *Smash*, sold over 4 million copies, making it "the best-selling indie rock album ever" (*RS*, 2/9/95). But a closer look reveals they are typical punks after all. Their lyrics are vulgar, we can't print what their T-shirt says, and in concert, every other word is the "F" word. They go out of their way to antagonize the establishment: "Parents are easy to piss off, so that's always fun to do," claims Dexter Holland, the band's singer/songwriter/guitarist. "And we did this record to piss off conservative Jerry Falwell America. That whole culture, the religious right, is just so full of s***" (*RIP*, 10/94).

For all their higher education, Offspring only contributes to the dumbing down of America. After all, "L.A. punk is mostly a bunch of smart kids pretending that they're dumb kids" (*SPIN*, 3/95). Punkers believe they are rugged individualists who think for themselves and refuse to conform to society's norms. But they haven't figured out that they all conform to the same rebellion. Nowhere is this more evident than at an Offspring concert, where thousands of kids flock to a concert of the most popular punk band in America. And together they all join in singing the latest individualist anthem: "*I'm not a trendy asshole!*" Maybe it's just blindness. "The god of this world has blinded the minds of the unbelieving, that they might not see the light of the gospel of the glory of Christ" (2 Cor. 4:4, NAS).

Music Exchange: Black Cherry Soda, the Blamed, Blenderhead, Crashdog, Crux, Focused, MxPx

ONYX

The boyz in this hip-hop quintet from Queens are all bald, despite the fact that they are all in their twenties. The look contributes to the hardened street-gang image they want to project. "We run around with bald heads because we rebels, ya know what I'm sayin'? Our music's about frustration and anger! That's why our logo is an angry face". (*SPIN*, 6/93). Their debut album, *Bacdafucup* (1993), was produced by Jam Master Jay of Run D.M.C. The album's hit single, "Slam," introduced the rap crowd to the chaos of slammin', (which originated in the punk pits as slam dancing and was modified by the metal crowd into moshing). In September, 1993, the band was arrested with Dr. Dre on the *Chronic* tour for stealing a van at gunpoint.

Their tough-guy image appeals to teenaged boys who want to feel powerful and invulnerable to the painful side of life. "We're ruder, nastier, blunter, more obnoxious—more everything than everybody else. That's just part of our appeal" (*LAT*, 11/21/93). They claim their music releases pent-up anger, but it only reinforces the rage. They're long on pointing out all the problems in life but short on solutions. They're only reinforcing the hate they say they hate.

> "*P*arents are easy to piss off, so that's always fun to do. And we did this record to piss off conservative Jerry Falwell America. That whole culture, the religious right, is just so full of s***."
> - **Dexter Holland of Offspring**

Music Exchange: Apocalypse, Gospel Ganstas, L.P.G., Preachas, S.F.C.

Ozzy OSBOURNE

Originally the singer for **Black Sabbath**, Ozzy left in 1979 to pursue a solo career. Albums like *Blizzard of Oz* (1980), *Diary of a Madman* (1981), and *Speak of the Devil* (1982) perpetuated the myth of Ozzy as the crazy satanist. It was reinforced by stunts like biting the head off a dove in front of record company executives and trying to bite off the head of a bat at a concert. Rumors of an Ozzy/Black Sabbath reunion tour in 1990 never materialized. Ozzy continued to record albums into the 1990s, but his antics seemed archaic and almost tame, compared to the death and destruction of death metal bands today. Although he keeps threatening to quit touring, he went back out on the road one more time in 1995 for his "Retirement Sucks" tour.

While Ozzy's image may have been wildly successful, his personal life was not. Most of his most outlandish pranks and stunts were the result of drug- and alcohol-induced insanity. He took LSD every day for two years while in Sabbath. The plane crash in 1982 that killed his talented young guitar player, Randy Rhodes, was the result of a stupid stunt gone wrong. In 1984, he was sued by the father of Ian McCallum, who committed suicide while listening to Ozzy's song "Suicide Solution." (The case was dropped because it couldn't be proven that the record made the boy kill himself.) He was also sued by his wife and manager, Sharon Arden, for spouse abuse.

Realizing that his alcohol problem had gotten out of hand, Ozzy was on and off the wagon for years before he claims he heard the voice of God tell him, "Quit today or you will die!" Staying sober has made the aging rocker far less threatening these days. While it cannot be proven that Ozzy ever took Satanism seriously, there is no question that he influenced thousands of teens to explore the occult and other dangerous behaviors, while trying to live up to the image of their hero.

Music Exchange: Mastadon, Shout, Rev Seven

PANTERA

These tough guys from Texas (*pantera* is Spanish for "panther") formed in 1983 doing Judas Priest covers. They've grown heavier and angrier with every album, starting with *Cowboys from Hell* (1990) and *Vulgar Display of Power* (1992). The group is fronted by lead screamer Phil Anselmo, who openly admits his passion for pot and professional boxing. "Never has a vocalist captured such rage, such bitterness, such bile in a performance. Listen to him sing 'F-ing Hostile' and tell me he doesn't mean it!" (*MM*, 8/92). *Far Beyond Driven* (1994) went to #1 on the charts the first week it was released. The album is full of brutal sexuality ("*I f—-ed your girlfriend last night / While you snored and drooled, I f—ed your love*" from "Good Friends and a Bottle of Pills"); suicide ("*I of Suicide / I, the Unlord / I'm born again with snake's eyes*" from "Becoming"); and drug use ("*But I'm helping to legalize dope on your pristine streets / And I'm making a fortune*" from "Strength Beyond Strength").

Their contempt of Christianity comes out in songs like "Throes of Rejection": "*If there really is a god / Then it's punishing me constantly*"; and "Hard Line, Sunken Cheeks": "*Simply to thy Ghost I reject / Simply to thy Ghost I give spit / Tempter, tempting, tempt me / You know that I'll submit / For this is my weakness / And it saves me—from those Christians.* "Something I find unbelievably stupid is putting the fear of God into kids' heads," Anselmo rails. "Making him watch his every footstep his whole life, to cater to an afterlife, when people need to figure out problems *today*. Gimme a break!" (*MM*, 8/92).

These guys are definitely angry about something. Perhaps a clue lies in the song "25 Years," where Anselmo rages against his father: "*I vent my frustration at you, old man - Drunken liar! / Orphaned by the dope and the drinks / I learned my lessons well / But the years of detachment have left me with demons now surfacing.*" A lot of kids are angry with absent fathers and neglectful mothers, and that's why this stuff sells. But to package that rage and sell it, just to play it over and over again is a pathetic waste of time. No one gets better feeding the fires of hatred and revenge. No one gets better until they discover the value of forgiveness. Any other advise is foolish: "Reckless words pierce like a sword, but the tongue of the wise brings healing; a fool is hotheaded and reckless; fools mock at making amends for sin; a wise son brings joy to his father, but a foolish man despises his mother; fools despise wisdom and discipline; the fool says in his heart, 'There is no God.' " (Prov. 12:18, 14:16b, 14:9a, 15:20, 1:7b, Psalm 14:1, NIV).

Music Exchange: The Blamed, the Crucified, Everdown, Focused, Precious Death, Six Feet Deep, Wish for Eden

PEARL JAM
••
Let's start with a short history lesson: The original Seattle grunge band was the now-defunct Green River (named after a local Seattle-area serial killer). Band members split up and went on to form two other Seattle bands, Mudhoney and Mother Love Bone. Mudhoney has gradually become more visible in the Seattle scene, but disaster struck Mother Love Bone just as they were about to release their first album (*Apple*, 1990). Their lead singer died of a heroin overdose at the age of 24 (*RS*, 5/3/90). A tribute album to him (*Temple of the Dog*, 1991) was released, which featured members of Soundgarden and ex-MLB members Jeff Ament and Stone Gossard. Meanwhile Eddie Vedder, a surfer from San Diego, found his way to Seattle via some demo tapes. Being major basketball fans, Ament, Gossard, and Vedder first called their band Mookie Blaylock (after the New Jersey Nets point guard whose number was 10). But they settled on Pearl Jam, based on Vedder's great-grandmother, Pearl, who allegedly made a special paste out of the drug peyote known as Pearl's jam.

Their first album, *Ten* (1991), sold over 6 million copies and stayed on the charts for almost two years. It came out right after **Nirvana's** *Nevermind,* opening up the rock world to all things grunge. Exposure as a fictional Seattle band called Citizen Dick in the movie *Singles* (1992) and a featured spot on the Lollapalooza tour helped rocket the band to popularity. The album featured the MTV video hit "Jeremy," about a child who commits suicide in his classroom because *"Daddy didn't give attention / To the fact that Mommy didn't care."* The video/song inspired several copy-cat suicides, including an 11-year-old who shot himself in front of his elementary school in Los Angeles. After winning the MTV award for best video, Vedder said, "If it wasn't for music, I would have shot myself in front of that classroom" (*RS*, 10/28/93).

The next album, *Vs.* (meaning versus or against, 1993), did even better, selling almost a million copies the first week. This album featured more social/political commentary than the first one, including songs about gun control ("Glorified G"), society's dominance by white males ("W.M.A."), and the anti-parental "Leash." By this time Vedder was heavily into an anti-rock-hero syndrome and refused to create hit singles or videos for the project. Despite his best efforts, the album went on to sell over 5 million copies. *Vitology* followed in 1994, with more of the same tortured look at relationships, betrayal, and suicide. The album also includes reprints of a bizarre pre-New Age text on Vitology (the study of life).

Kids relate to Vedder's songs of frustration and confusion, especially about relationships and family. (Vedder fought constantly with his dad and learned later that the man was not his real father. By the time he found out about his real father, the man had died of multiple sclerosis.) His popularity pegs him as a spokesman for Generation X, but Vedder is a somewhat reluctant rock hero. "Think about it, man. Any generation that would pick Kurt (Cobain of Nirvana) or me as its spokesman, that must be a pretty screwed up generation, don't you think?" He went on in that interview to confess that he doesn't have the answers his fans are searching for (*SDU*, 6/8/94).

But this hasn't kept him from offering his opinions anyway. After the release of *Vs.*, Pearl Jam resisted the rock star syndrome by playing smaller venues and taking on the ticket agency Ticketmaster for its inflated ticket prices. They jumped on the pro-abortion bandwagon by playing for several of L7's Rockers for Choice benefit concerts. "We have to ensure the protection of women's reproductive rights," says Vedder, "and the safety of our mothers and sisters" (*BG*, 1/11/95). (There's no mention of how to ensure the safety of the child growing in the womb.) And (get this logic) while it's perfectly alright to abort babies, it's absolutely criminal what they're doing to frogs these days. Vedder joined PETA (People for the Ethical Treatment of Animals) to protest the unethical treatment of the poor amphibians in high school biology labs all across the country. They set up an 800-number so students could voice their desire to "cut out dissection" from the curriculum (*APN*, 2/20/95).

Vedder seems like a humble hero to his fans. But there's a kind of arrogance in being so sure that no one can be sure of anything. The only thing he believes in is the music. "Music—this is my religion. I get joy from it" (*APN*, 1/16/95). "There should be no messiahs in music. The music itself, I don't mind worshipping that" (*RS*, 10/28/93). He's right about musical messiahs. All the world's heroes will let you down at some point, and so will the music. It is, after all, the creation of creatures, not the Creator Himself. "Satan's Bed" (*"I'll wait for angels / but I won't hold my breath / Imagine they're busy / I'm doin' okay"*) and "Tremor Christ" express Vedder's belief that faith in anything but his music is a shaky proposition. Perhaps if Vedder took his eyes off the floor and off his own tortured feelings, to look up for just a moment, he might see what a real Messiah looks like.

Music Exchange: Applehead, Grammatrain, Plank Eye, Sometime Sunday, Yonderboy, Wish for Eden

Liz PHAIR

This native of Chicago is relatively new to the college radio scene. Her debut album, *Exile in Guyville* (1994), was deliberately designed to parallel the Rolling Stone's *Exile on Main Street.* The aggressive sexuality expressed in her album has her being touted as a feminist spokesperson. She says her favorite pastimes are smoking pot and "chick" watching (*RS,* 10/14/93). The album package features photos of the singer in various stages of undress. The lyrics are full of frank sexuality. But this is not the seductive tease of an R&B girl group or the perverted experimentation of Madonna. Phair propositions her partners with all the finesse of a bulldozer in songs like "F*** and Run" and "Flower" (*"I'll f*** you 'til your d*** turns blue!).*

But there's more going on here than vulgar sexuality. She's been praised for her "refreshingly angry and aggressive attitude toward men and sex" (*NW,* 3/28/94), and she's become a symbol of liberation to the "empower women" crowd. All this may make her seem politically correct, but it makes her socially and spiritually wrong. If these crude come-ons are considered sexist and deameaning when they come from a man (and they should be), why are they considered "refreshing" when they come from a woman? Bitterness and revenge may be good enough reasons for those in the world, but they're inadequate excuses for those in the Kingdom. And nothing constructive comes of it. Those who are obsessed with power and revenge become just like the people they hate (Rom. 8:29).

Music Exchange: Hoi Polloi, Riki Michelle

PORNO FOR PYROS

Perry Farrell (not his real name, it's a pun on the word *peripheral*) originally played in a short-lived band called Psi-Com in 1981, which dissolved over "religious differences"—Farrell was reportedly getting into black magic, while the rest of the band became Hare Krishnas. Farrell formed Jane's Addiction in 1986, drawing as much attention for his album covers as for his music. *Nothing's Shocking* (1988), featured one of Farrell's shocking works of "art": a pair of nude Siamese twins sitting in a rocking chair with their hair on fire! The second album, *Ritual de lo Habitual* (1991) featured his artwork of three semi-nude paper mache figures surrounded by pseudo-religious curios. Farrell claims the piece was based on a sexual experience he had with a couple of women in New York.

Farrell has no compunctions about exposing such ideas to young people: "They'll see that it's possible for three people to lay in bed, and it may inspire them to try it. What's wrong with that?" (*Daily Bulletin*, 1/5/91). He also maintains that drug use is a positive, creative act and is quite public about his use of heroin, hash, and peyote. He is fascinated by bizarre religions and the occult. The religious look of the *Ritual* album actually reflects his interest in Santeria—an occult mix of voodoo and Catholicism. He flew to Mexico to marry his girlfriend in a Santeria ceremony and was reportedly keeping live chickens in his apartment for sacrifice.

Amid rumors that he had AIDS, Farrell disbanded Jane's Addiction in 1991. His farewell tour was a traveling rock-n-roll circus called the Lollapalooza Festival. It's a showcase for new bands, social/environmental causes, and a bizarre collection of artists, fashions, and perversions that makes P. T. Barnum's freak show look like an afternoon tea party. "Florescent colors, Beavis and Butthead, teenagers sniffing glue—this is Lollapalooza in a nutshell. Complete decadence!" (*SPIN*, 11/94). The festival became an annual event and Farrell started a new band in 1993. "Porno for Pyros follows the same path as his previous band, combining art rock, punk, heavy metal, and funk into one shrieking whole" (*AMG*, pg. 253).

Farrell pontificates on everything as if he's the first guy to have discovered thought, but his logic is twisted by drugs and savaged by selfishness. He offers his fans nothing but misdirected anger and neo-psychedelic chaos. He lives in absolute defiance of everyone and everything, except his own self-destructive choices. To the naive rock addict, Farrell might seem like some kind of rock-n-roll visionary guru. But any Jane or Johnny who becomes addicted to his drug-infused double-speak will only end up dead—spiritually, morally, and/or literally.

Music Exchange: Breakfast With Amy, Dig Hay Zoose, Hot Pink Turtle, poor old lu, Scattered Few

PUBLIC ENEMY
This rap group bridges the gap between the B-boy braggin' of early rap and the violent misogyny of the gansta scene. Their aggressive black nationalism and militant imagery earned them a reputation as the "Black Panthers of Rap." Group members Chuck D. and Professor Griff began

115

hosting music programs together in New York in 1979, forming Public Enemy in 1986. Their first album (*Yo! Bum Rush The Show*, 1987) created a stir in both the white and black communities with fist-in-your-face tunes like "Public Enemy No. 1" and "Mi-uzi Weighs A Ton." It was followed by *It Takes A Nation Of Millions To Hold Us Back* (1989), considered by some the best hip-hop album ever made.

During their first concert tour, they used the Security of the First World—an all-Muslim band of bodyguards dressed in para-military camouflage who carried Uzi machine guns. "Bring On the Noise" endorsed radical Black Muslim leader Louis Farrakhan, who is often criticized for anti-Semitism and reverse racism. Professor Griff was fired from the group when he claimed that Jews were "responsible for the majority of wickedness that goes on across the globe" (*WT*, 5/22/89). He was reinstated a few months later after the furor died down.

Fear of a Black Planet (1990) and *Apocalypse 91...The Enemy Strikes Back* (1991) offered the same themes with diminishing returns. By this time, Flavor Flav (he's the one with the oversized clock hanging around his neck) had become visible as the concert's comedy relief. (His personal life was anything but funny, as he's been arrested on several occasions for assault during arguments with his lover—the mother of his three children, *LAT*, 11/2/93). The album *Muse Sick N Hour Mess Age* (1994) was panned by fans and critics alike. Although Public Enemy's musical prowess has begun to diminish, their political prowess has not. Chuck D. is still considered a valid spokesman for the black nation.

Public Enemy is not an easy analysis. Their views on injustice and the greedy self-interests of the world are not entirely without merit. But how do we respond to those who embrace a form of Islam that considers whites and Christians as pagan infidels? Is Christ politically liberal or conservative? These are not simple questions to answer. However, the bottom line for Public Enemy is power—black power. To believe that solutions for our lives lie in any power but God's power is to shortchange Him and our faith. To believe that any power will prove to be more effective than God's is to miss what it means to place your trust in Him in the first place. Unless we surrender to His power, we all become our own worst enemy.

Music Exchange: Apocalypse, L.P.G., Preachas, S.F.C.

RANCID

Move over **Green Day** and **Offspring**, the new punk kids on the block have arrived. Hailing from the same San Francisco-area punk club that gave birth to Green Day (Gilman Street in Berkeley), these guys are bringing back every punk craze from mohawks to moshing. Their music is a unique blend of hard-core punk and ska (a melodic offshoot of reggae), bringing them comparisons to the original classic punk band, the Clash. Their self-titled debut album in 1993 and *Let's Go* (1994) were both produced on the independent record label, Epitaph (Offspring's label which is owned by Bad Religion). The albums were popular enough to court some big contracts from major labels, but in the end they decided to stay with Epitaph for their latest release, *And Out Come The Wolves.*

The band's singer/founder, Tim Armstrong (no relation to Green Day's Billy Armstrong), was brought up in an impoverished childhood, complete with abusive, alcoholic father. After a bout with drugs and alcohol himself, Armstrong cleaned up through the Salvation Army and decided to form the band. Although he seems to be staying clean and sober, he isn't exactly a poster-boy for abstinence. "I ain't no (expletive) role model—how could I be? I don't think drinking's bad; I don't think drugs are bad. I just think if you're going to die from it, you might want to stop" (*LAT,* 9/3/95). He's also been exposed to the gospel, but that doesn't seem to have impacted him either. In the song "Holiday Sunrise," he says: *"Relatives of mine said they were born again / F***ed up world has made me born against / I'm a sinner and my soul should be cleansed / But I'll take my chances when I'm dead."* There's no better example of the principle of Colossians 2:8. Listening to Rancid will *spoil* your faith and joy in Jesus Christ.

Music Exchange: Black Cherry Soda, MxPx, One Bad Pig

R.E.M.

....

This college radio favorite blended accessible pop sounds with post-punk sensibilities, persisting until it brought post-modern rock into the mainstream. They began in the college town of Athens, Georgia in 1980. Initially part of the nouveau hippie Paisley Underground movement, they called themselves R.E.M. (for Rapid Eye Movement in deep sleep) to show what deep dreamers they were. The catchy sounds of their first single "Radio Free Europe" (1981) brought comparisons to the Byrds. Their first album, *Murmur* (1983), was a critical favorite, but Michael Stipes' mumbled vocals and indecipherable lyrics kept them out of Top 40 radio.

Document (1987) was their breakthrough album with hits like "The One I Love" and "It's the End of the World As We Know It (and I Feel Fine)"—perhaps because the lyrics were finally becoming intelligible. *Green* (1988) gave us the "Stand," which became the theme song of Chris Elliot's short-lived TV show. *Out of Time* (1991) yeilded the controversial hit "Losing My Religion." *Automatic For The People* (1992) was a sadly melodic album with brooding ruminations on losses of all sorts. *Monster* (1994) hit the top of the charts with the help of the video "What's the Frequency, Kenneth?"

While R.E.M.'s songs have sometimes been hard to decipher, they are clear about other issues. Members of Greenpeace, they support just about every liberal social/political cause in the books: abortion, the environment, anti-nuke, PETA, etc. "My job in rock music," claimed Stipes on MTV in 1989, "is to make political activism sexy." Stipe's sexual orientation has also been called into question lately. After a long affair with Natalie Merchant of 10,000 Maniacs, there are indications that Stipe has become more experimental sexually. During a brief affair with Kurt Cobain's widow, **Courtney Love**, he encouraged her to explore sex with other women (*VF,* 6/95). In an interview for "Extra" (6/95), he side-stepped questions about his homosexuality, by suggesting that sexual orientation doesn't matter.

I disagree with those who claim that "Losing My Religion" is an anti-Christian song. I don't think it gets that far. You can't lose what you never had. What Stipe and his fans struggle with is losing themselves and losing their faith in love and even reality itself. Losing is a big issue for this lost generation, and it's no wonder. They keep following blind guides and false prophets. That's why Jesus said, "I am the Way and the Truth and the Life...Come to Me all who are weary and heavy-laden, and I will give you rest" (John 14:6, Matt.11:28, NAS).

Music Exchange: Adam Again, Black Eyed Sceva, the Choir, Hocus Pick, Lost Dogs, the Throes, the Waiting, Walter Eugenes, Villanelle

Henry ROLLINS

By day, Rollins worked in a dead-end job as an ice cream store clerk. By night, he toured the punk clubs of Washington, D.C., looking for a raging slam-pit. "I lived for those shows," he says. "Violence was my girl. Getting into fistfights, smelling blood, breaking noses—that was my high, my woman. I got beat up and I beat other people up" (*LAT*, 6/14/87). Then in 1981, he was asked to sing for L.A.'s angriest punk band, Black Flag.

For the next five years, Rollins raged on stage, carrying the crucible of punk anger to disenfranchised youth everywhere. "Black Flag took a look around their sun-drenched hometown and got pissed—pissed about the suntans, pissed about suburban decadence, pissed for the sake of being pissed. Henry Rollins expressed the nihilism, cynicism and outrage of suburban youths better than any of his hardcore peers" (*AMG*, pg. 40). Ever the rugged individualist, Rollins wore his hair long, when everyone else in punk had a mohawk or was a skinhead, leaving him looking like some kind of psychotic punk version of Charles Manson. It ended in 1986, because the band's founder, Gregg Ginn had grown weary of the gig and too busy with SST, the successful independent record company he'd founded.

> "**V**iolence was my girl. Getting into fistfights, smelling blood, breaking noses— that was my high, my woman. I got beat up and I beat other people up."
> — *Henry Rollins*

But Rollins was not one to sit idle. He was producing spoken-word albums and books of his own peculiar brand of aggressive punk poetry before the band ever broke up. Rollins jumped into the poetry circuits, which led to a revival of the beat-poet movement of the late 1950s. By 1987, he'd already started his own hardcore outfit called the Rollins Band.

As alternative music and hardcore emerged from the underground in the early '90s, Rollins' status began to change from punk pariah to Mr. Media Savvy. He hosted MTV's *Alternative Nation*, appeared on Dennis Miller's short-lived talk show, showed up on some PBS specials, and even did ads for the Gap and Apple computers. He's also started a minor movie career with roles in *The Chase* (1994) with Charlie Sheen and *Johnny Mnemonic* (1995) with Keanu Reeves.

Rollins is not a typical punk. On the human level, there are even some things to admire about him. He does not do drugs, drink alcohol, or smoke (his main vice seems to be coffee.) He does not use profanity on his albums. He's health conscious enough to avoid red meat and disciplined enough to work out with weights an hour each day. He is intelligent, articulate, and well read. Unlike most of the whiners and screamers out there, Rollins does not seek to blame and destroy his world. He looks for constructive solutions—solutions that are admittedly limited by his humanistic philosophy.

Rollins is what most punks only pretend to be—a genuine individualist. Unlike most rockers, he is not dependent on others for his sense of independence. He is not bound by corporate convention or punk conformity. He produces his books through his own publishing company (called *2.13.61,* derived from his birthdate), which he runs from his house.

He is a tireless worker, rejecting the slacker attitude of his peers: "I don't know about these 'heroes' today. These people should get themselves to a gym with all due speed, watch their diets, start standing straighter, get the greasy hair out of their face and stop trying to be famous for being a couch potato who plays good music. My thing has always been: Get up, get into it, get involved, not drop and tune out. What are you doing slacking? The world's on fire! For me the '90s are a call to arms" (*R.S.,* 1/6/94). (God help us, but he's starting to sound like Al Menconi or someone's dad!)

But Rollins does have one huge flaw. While he is fiercely independent, he is also fiercely angry. If there is a single word that defines him, it is **rage.** "Rage is to Rollins as snow is to Eskimos. He knows its textures so intimately that he has 40 different ways to describe it" (*LAT,* 3/8/92). That fire is fueled by a physically abusive father, whom he has not spoken to since he was 18. He also finds inspiration for his fury in the senseless death of a close friend.

Rollins claims he writes and speaks and screams on stage to get the rage out of him, but somehow he has missed the principle of reinforcement. He has rehearsed his rage for so long, it has become the only identity he knows. He tries to use anger to find his freedom, but it has become his prison. He will never find resolution by simply rehearsing his rage. There is no peace without forgiveness. Unless Rollins reconciles with the Father and forgives his father, he will carry the fire of his anger and alienation into the most fiery and alienated place in the universe—the ultimate mosh pit of Hell.

Music Exchange: Fell Venus, Focused, Nobody Special, Undercover

SALT-N-PEPA

Salt (Cheryl James) and Pepa (Sandra Denton) were working at Sears when their supervisor, Hurby "Luv Bug" Azor, asked them to help him with a record he was doing for a college class. The result was a tune called "Showstopper" (a response to Doug E. Fresh's "The Show") and it got an "A" with audiences as it sold 250,000 copies and hit the Top 20 on the black charts. Although there were other women in rap, Salt-N-Pepa became the first female crew to put out an entire rap album, *Hot, Cool, and Vicious* in 1987. The sexy single from that album, "Push It" caused quite a furor at a California high school when the cheerleaders used it for a routine at a game (*Rancho Cordova Independent,* 3/19/88). Their second album, *A Salt With a Deadly Pepa,* contained a variety of music styles including reggae, dance, and a ballad. Their third album contained a frank "safe-sex" primer called "Let's Talk About Sex." In 1994, the single they recorded with **En Vogue**, "Whatta Man," went straight to the top of the charts.

When Salt-N-Pepa arrived on the scene, female rappers were just a novelty act. By doing some "pushing" of their own, they opened the doors for other females rappers like Queen Latifa, Yo-Yo, Monie Love, and MC Lyte. They began as a street-tough, B-girl crew to combat the macho/sexist attitudes of male rappers (they refer to guys who cheat on their girlfriends as "tramps"). Their message focused on self-esteem and sexual independence for women. "Despite the graphic sexual overtones in some of their lyrics, they still come off as strong, independent ladies of the '80s." Or as the group's DJ, Spinderella (Dee Roper), put it, "We're showing all of those guys that we can be just as hard, just as def as they can, and still be proud to be females" (*BB,* 2/89).

Unfortunately, Salt-N-Pepa have not kept their street image entirely intact. As they've grown older (and more attractive), their image has grown softer and more seductive. They've started using sex as a weapon by giving it as a prize or withholding it as punishment, as it suits them. However, none of this ultimately works well in honest relationships. Neither sex nor insults are an adequate substitute for self-esteem. Although we understand the temptation to "do unto men as they have done unto you," seductive manipulation and macha bullying won't work any better for women than it has for men. The key to personal power does not lie in sexual prowess or self-assertion but in selfless service to Jesus. A bond slave of Christ still has more power than the biggest boaster on the streets.

Music Exchange: Angi & Debi (Winans), MC Gee Gee, Out of Eden

SEAL
....

If Seal is distinct and unique as a musician, it is because he has such a wide variety of influences in his life. Sealhenry Samuel is the London-born son of a Nigerian father and Brazilian mother. His imposing appearance (he is 6'4") is somewhat humbled by deep scars in his cheeks, the remnants of a childhood disease. He has a degree in architecture and worked as a fashion designer, before trying his hand at music. Musical influences include **Bob Marley,** Joni Mitchell, Jimi Hendrix**,** and Crosby, Stills, Nash, and Young (an influence clearly heard on his hit "Kiss from a Rose," the love theme from the film *Batman Forever* in 1995). His music is a unique mix of pop, reggae, rock, R&B, and acid house dance music.

His lyrics are often vaguely spiritual, reflecting a wide variety of personal experiences. He spent time in the Far East and India where he "became much more aware of spirituality" (*LAT*, 3/22/92). A palm reader in New York predicted a series of personal trials for him—after which he caught double pneumonia, was almost killed in a car accident, and suffered a bout with chronic fatigue, which drove him to a faith healer in London. Even his goals for his music are a mix of selfish and humanitarian: "All my songs are therapy. I'm giving therapy to myself" (*RS*, 8/25/94); and "What's really important to me is that I become a good musician, that I write good songs, and that they affect people in a positive way" (*BB*, 4/92).

Seal projects an idealistic humanism that is attractive to many young Christians. "I believe the main cause of problems like war and racism is people's inability to communicate and hence to understand and respect each other's culture. Sadly, I don't have the answers to these questions, but one thing for sure is we are at the dawning of a new spiritual age of awareness and that complacency is becoming a thing of the past" (from the liner notes of his album *Seal,* 1994). Indeed, we would all benefit from better communication and more understanding. But to believe that we are on the edge of a new dawn is merely wishful thinking. What Seal sees is the result of the fallen nature of man, and that nature will not change by wishing it otherwise. Things won't change until *we* change, and we won't change until we submit our deepest selves to the character of Christ. Seal's music is humanly hopeful and positive, even spiritual, and that's a step in the right direction, but you won't find a complete picture of Christ's plan in the mix here.

Music Exchange: Clay House, DC Talk (*Jesus Freak*), Patsy Moore, Ben Okafor, Charlie Peacock, World Wide Message Tribe

SEX PISTOLS

This experiment in manipulation succeeded beyond anyone's wildest dreams. Malcolm McLaren, who owned a boutique in London called Sex, decided to see if could sell the public a band that was the exact opposite of the current crop of glitter rockers. He'd had some experience in the music business managing the outrageous cross-dressing band, the New York Dolls. One of McLaren's employees had a band that needed a singer. They chose an unpleasant young man named Johnny Lydon. He was renamed Johnny Rotten because of his poor dental hygiene (his teeth were actually green) and his reputation for rudeness.

They played for the first time in November, 1975. "While the band played loudly and abrasively, Rotten arrogantly sang of anarchy, violence, fascism, and apathy" (*AMG*, pg. 287). Their reputation spread like a fungus, and they were signed to EMI Records. Their first single, "Anarchy In The UK" (1976), caused such an outcry, EMI cancelled their contract days after its release. McLaren pocketed a sizeable advance and signed the band to A&M Records. They added John Ritchie to the band. (Rotten renamed him Sid Vicious after his pet hamster.) Within a month A&M also cancelled their contract. McLaren pocketed another advance. In 1977, they released the single "God Save the Queen" (just in time to mock the silver jubilee of Queen Elizabeth II) and the album *Never Mind The Bollocks*. Since no hall in England would book them, they left to tour America.

Playing throughout the Bible Belt, they braved death threats and riots. Vicious was addicted to heroin by this time and thought nothing of cutting himself open on stage. The bloody, abusive tour lasted 12 days. At the close of the show in San Francisco on January 14, 1978, Rotten announced the band was over. McLaren managed to squeeze a few more dollars out of his creation with the release of a couple of albums containing repackaged singles. Rotten left for New York, changed his name back to John Lydon, and formed the group PiL (Public Image Ltd).

Vicious wandered aimlessly with groupie girlfriend Nancy Spungen. He woke up one October (1978) morning in a heroin haze, and found Nancy dead, with his knife in her stomach. She was 20. He was arrested for her murder, but let out on bail. Before it came to trial, Vicious (who was only 21) overdosed and was found dead on February 2, 1979. A movie called *Sid & Nancy* (1986) made them into a kind of punk Romeo and Juliet, exploiting the tragedy while ignoring the deadly lessons.

Richard Hell of the New York punk band, the Voidoids, summarized it this way: "Sid's whole identity was self-destruction. He was famous for dying. It's all he knew how to do. For Sid and Nancy, there was no more exciting way to be young than to die before they grew up" (*SPIN*, 10/86). The band burned out in two short years, but it fueled the punk movement and crystalized the fury and futility of punk's self-destructive nihilism. But burying themselves in hollow rhetoric about anger and anarchy led to nothing but dead ends and bad ends. Living well, in Christ, *is* the best revenge, after all.

Music Exchange: the Blamed, Crashdog, the Crucified, Fluffy, MxPx, One Bad Pig

SILVERCHAIR
....

This is a young rock trio from Australia—and we do mean young. When they first hit big in America, they were all only 16, after already playing in their own country for two years. They found popularity with the grunge rock crowd with a sound somewhere between Pearl Jam and Helmet. They entered a local song contest in June, 1994 and won a chance to record professionally. The first song, "Tomorrow" went to #1 in Australia. The album *Frogstomp* (1995) followed and went platinum within a week.

Their lyrics are typical grunge fare which tends to avoid themes of sex in favor of some rather shallow social commentary (i.e., war is bad, suicide is scary, pollution is bad, drugs are scary, hatred is bad, etc.) "Every time I come up with a good idea for a song, it's about death," says singer/songwriter Daniel Johns (*RIP*, 12/95). The band is so young, their songs fail to reflect the intense anguish of Nirvana or Nine Inch Nails, but what else would we expect from a band who's been managed by their mothers? Teenage boys will identify with them just because they're young, and girls are attracted to them because they're cute—sort of a grunge New Kids on the Block.

While it's hard to criticize a band this enthusiastic and naive, they still fail to bring anyone closer to Christ. And the innocence won't last. It will disappear into cynical bitterness so common among their musical peers. And as Margaret Becker reminds us—once lost, it is impossible to recapture our innocence without Christ.

Music Exchange: Grammatrain, Precious Death, Sometime Sunday, Wish for Eden

SKINNY PUPPY

This is a Canadian trio led by head howler Nivek Ogre (real name: Kevin Ogilvie). They started out doing performance-art set to synthesized noise rock back in 1983. Albums like *Mind: The Perpetual Intercourse* (1986) and *Rabies* (1988) made them underground favorites. The album *Too Dark Park* is typical of the band's demented mindset: "This album is Skinny Puppy's return to the bloodbath. Dark shadows lurk everywhere, just the way the band likes it. You can be a 'spun web, deluded of life' or a 'crushed velvet corpse,' because with Skinny Puppy, every day is Halloween" (*SPIN*, 2/91). For a number of years, Ogre's massive cocaine and heroin habits added to the paranoia and rage of the band's message. He eventually

> **"Sid's whole identity was self-destruction. He was famous for dying. It's all he knew how to do. For Sid and Nancy, there was no more exciting way to be young than to die before they grew up."**
> **- on Sid Vicious of the Sex Pistols**

cleaned up to survive, but Dwayne Goettel, the groups keyboard/drum machine programmer, did not. He died of a heroine overdose in August, 1995 at his parent's home at the age of 31, while the band was working on their ninth album. The group's future is now uncertain.

Borrowing liberally from **Alice Cooper**'s school of Shock Rock, Skinny Puppy's demented stage show has included the simulated mutilation of baby dolls and small animals. They often play their music while scenes from slasher and snuff films are played on huge backdrop screens behind them. "I love covering myself in blood every night," Ogre claims. "I love putting things over my head that I can tear off. No matter how sick and twisted it all is, I totally get into it" (*AP*, 7/92).

If **Ministry** reflects the anger and angst of the anguished soul, Skinny

Puppy is the sinister voice that beckons them into that dark night. They reflect the cry of the eternal victim. Skinny Puppy represents ". . .a cornered animal; the mute animal that can't speak up, but when its tail gets stepped on, it screams" (*RIP,* 1/93). But like their stage show, their perception of themselves is a delusion. Ogre sees himself as a tortured victim, but on stage he glorifies the torturer and the victimizer. He teaches his fans to deal with their pain by reveling in the delicious agony of it all. And whether he realizes it or not, he acts as the Devil's agent, by selling front row seats to his brutal vision of Hell. "So it will be at the end of the age; the angels shall come forth, and take out the wicked from among the righteous, and will cast them into the furnace of fire; there shall be weeping and gnashing of teeth" (Matt. 13:49-50, NAS).

Music Exchange: Brainchild/Circle of Dust, Fell Venus, Global Wave System, Mortal, X-Propagation

SLAYER.

This thrash metal quartet formed in Los Angeles in 1982. In the early days there were plenty of pentagrams and upside-down crosses, and lots of stage blood splattered everywhere, making them the new leaders of Black Metal mania. The EP *Haunting the Chapel* depicted demons taking over the church and burning heaven down. *Hell Awaits* (1985) was "a smorgasbord of satanic worship, violent death, and brutal rape. The song 'Kill Again,' for example, details the murderous deeds of a schizophrenic lunatic: *'Slice her flesh to shreds / Watch the blood run free.'* The rest of the album deals with the gates of hell, the tombs of hell, the fiery pits of hell, and other related topics" (*HP,* 4/85). They continued this brutal, demonic direction on *Reign In Blood* (1987) and *South of Heaven* (1988) with tunes about torture ("Behind the Crooked Cross" and "Angel of Death"), satanic rituals ("Cleanse the Soul" and "Spill the Blood"), sex with the dead ("Necrophilic" and "Necrophobic"), and mockery of Christ in "Jesus Saves."

When CBS Records refused to distribute their occultic material, they were picked up by Rick Rubin of Def Jam, who produces rappers like **Public Enemy** and metal acts like **Danzig.** Other than a change of drummers in 1992 and guitarist Kerry King cutting his hair, Slayer remains the same. *Decade of Aggression* (1992) highlights ten years of their deadly music. The title tune on *Divine Intervention* (1994) makes God out to be a heartless monster on Judgement Day. There's a chilling portrait of serial killers like Jeffrey Dahmer in "213." The song "Dittohead" reflects a Limbaugh-like perspective on the corruption of society and the rise of

126

savagery—as if Slayer never contributed to this condition in America.

Slayer once claimed to be real Satanists, but now they admit it was all a marketing ploy. Christian talk-show host Bob Larson went behind the scenes on their 1988 tour, but failed to find any evidence of true Satanism. "Slayer doesn't serve Satan," he concluded. "They bow before the teen who won't buy their next record if they aren't evil enough" (*SPIN*, 5/89). Still, they've managed to usher many of their fans into the dark realms. Typically, Slayer just blames the parents: "I think (our music) does affect neglected people, but it's not our fault they're neglected. Their parents won't relate to them, so kids relate to us" (*Cornerstone*, Issue 88). That may be so, but how does dwelling on death and despair or peering into pits of hell help their lonely, troubled fans? It doesn't (see Col. 3:1-2). Satanism aside, Slayer is still one of the best examples of the principle: if you're not part of the solution, you're part of the problem.

Music Exchange: Bloodshed, Mortification, Testament, Unashamed

SMASHING PUMPKINS
....

This Chicago quartet formed in 1988, and produced their first album, *Gish* (1991), on an independent record label. The album won critical acclaim and got them a major label contract, but the attention and fame nearly tore the band apart. Drummer Jimmy Chamberlain developed serious drug and alcohol problems, guitarist James Iha and (female) bassist D'Arcy broke up as a couple, and the band's leader, Billy Corgan, had a mental breakdown: "Here I am going along in life, I'm suicidal, completely depressed, I hate myself, I hate my band" (*SPIN*, 11/93). Nevertheless, they managed to produce a second album, *Siamese Dream* (1993), which has sold nearly 4 million copies.

Pisces Iscariot (1994), an album of B-sides (leftover songs), was released to keep fans happy while they worked on their next album—a 28-song, 2-CD collection called *Mellon Collie and the Infinite Sadness* (1995). It's an eclectic mix of classical nocturne (the title tune), fusion rock ("Tonight, Tonight"), synthesized pop ("Porcelina of the Vast Oceans"), punk fury ("Tales Of A Scorched Earth"), and gloomy death rock ("Here is No Why") which has earned them comparisons to Yes at its most ostentatious.

Their lyrics are murky and generally make little sense. What bits and pieces do make sense, (lyrics like: "*Love is suicide,*" "*Intoxicated with the madness / I'm in love with my sadness,*" and "*Despite all my rage, I'm just a rat in a cage / And I know that I'll never be saved*") reveal a resigned sense of hopelessness. "Corgan's lyrics are definitely post-punk, detailing depression and angst" (*AMG*, pg. 295).

Musically, Corgan is quite talented—he writes, arranges, sings, and plays guitar, keyboards and bass. He's also profoundly confused and lost. "I've never had a stable life," says Corgan. "I lived in five different places before I was 5. I saw divorces, messy breakups, boyfriends, girlfriends, drugs. I don't trust stability. I understand chaos. I muck things up on purpose because it forces you to react. I don't understand what it is to have everyone like you and think you're great" (*CT*, 10/23/93). Although it's a mystery to most adults, many young people identify with all this madness and aimless agonizing. "The Pumpkin's audience is probably as dysfunctional as the band itself. Corgan's profoundly conflicted lyrical persona speaks clearly to the 20-somethings, a generation born of broken homes, lousy schools, and diminished opportunities" (*RS*, 10/14/93).

But Smashing Pumpkins isn't healing souls. Despite the apparent vulnerability and raw emotion in this type of alternative music, it is actually rather heartless and cruel. It offers no hope for the hopeless, no comfort for the suffering, and no way out of the pit of despair. This broken generation needs to spend less time detailing the agony of their lives, and more time developing solutions for their ills. And if Jesus is not at the heart of these reflections, the alternative does indeed look bleak.

Music Exchange: Art Core, Dig Hay Zoose, Luxury, poor old lu, Plank Eye, Prayer Chain, Raspberry Jam, Starflyer 59

SOUL ASYLUM
••

Although Soul Asylum is considered one of the new alternative bands on the circuit, they were actually doing the plaid/grunge thing a decade before the Seattle scene sub-popped into view. The band formed in 1981 in Minneapolis, part of the area's roots-rock revival that also spawned Hüsker Dü and the Replacements. In fact, Hüsker Dü's Bob Mould produced their first two albums. They toured the country with their punk-edged rock, as an underground college-radio favorite throughout the 1980s.

After a decade of doing rock the hard way, they finally got noticed on a national scale for their hit song "Runaway Train" from the album *Grave Dancer's Union* (1992). A video for the song became an MTV staple during the summer of 1993, because it featured photos of missing runaway teens. MTV also offered a promo with an 800- number for runaways to call for help to get back home. As a result, several teens in the U.S. and England were restored to their families. During this time, Dave Pirner (the group's singer/songwriter/guitarist) also got some attention as actress Winona Rider's main squeeze. The trend to accessibility continued on *Let Your Dim Light Shine* (1995), with it's MTV video hit "Just Like

Anyone." This pop-rock tune illustrates the value of self-acceptance as the video depicts a miserable young lady who literally finds her wings.

Pirner is as insightful and sensitive as a chain-smoking, beer-drinking rocker can be: "You can't change the past, but you can mess up a perfectly good present by worrying about the future." In fact, they are surprisingly unpretentious. They are unfazed by their better-late-than-never success. They refused to milk the plight of runaways as a stepping stone for their own success. "We're not authorities on this," admits Pirner honestly. "I never had an ulterior motive with this song. I know where I came from, and I'm old enough now that I have a perspective where I can't get caught up in the superficial nature of show business" (*LAT*, 10/3/93).

The music is not so much about anger or self-destruction as frustration and restlessness. There is even a tune called "Homesick" that is almost Christian in its longing for a better world: "*We are not of this world / And there's a place for us / Oh, I am so Homesick / I'm Homesick for the Home I've never had...*") Pirner admits he wants to influence people with his music: "I felt like Lou Reed was there for me when I was growing up...Dylan, Neil Young, all these people helped me learn more about myself, somehow, and I'm trying to return the favor" (*RIP*, 5/93). Actually, every artist in this book is trying to influence our children with their perspective on life. Most just aren't honest enough to admit it.

Music Exchange: Adam Again, Clash of Symbols, 77's, Third Day

SPIN DOCTORS
••

This rock band formed in 1989 at a New York City art school, frequently opening for their friends in the band Blues Traveler. Their debut album, *Pocket Full of Kryptonite* (1992), was going nowhere fast until a Vermont radio station used one of their songs in a commercial. Listener requests led to a stint on "Saturday Nite Live" and a surge in their popularity. Tie-dye shirts, a propensity for pot, and the group's extensive improvisational jams in concert have given them a reputation as the new **Grateful Dead** (*RS*, 1/7/93). Some of their music is fun and funky pop/rock, but their consistent use of pot and psychedelic philosophy doesn't commend itself to the Christian.

The Spin Doctors want to take us back to the free-wheeling '60s. Why? "The '60s was a really rich time," says singer Chris Barron. "Rock-n-roll was going down in biblical proportions. Bob Dylan, Jimi Hendrix...some heavy icons. I don't own a stereo, but I hear that stuff all the time. It's in my ear" (*Circus*, 6/93). Do we really need to revel in the '60s? That decade brought us LSD, Eastern mysticism, and free love, which is why we are wrestling with drug addiction, the New Age, and

AIDS today. The dawning of the Age of Aquarius had turned into a dark nightmare. Rather than look back into the purple haze of yesterday, we'd do better to look to the coming of Christ, when everything will become crystal clear.

Music Exchange: Raspberry Jam, Swirling Eddies

SPINAL TAP

Let's make this perfectly clear. *Spinal Tap is not a real band!* It is the name of a mythical group in Rob Reiner's clever film called *This Is Spinal Tap* (1984), about rock and roll excess. The trio is composed of vocalist David St. Hubbins (played by Michael McKean, best known as Lenny on "Laverne and Shirley"), guitarist Nigel Tufnel, and bassist Derek Smalls (Harry Shearer and Christopher Guest, both "Saturday Nite Live" veterans).

Starting with their early days as a Mercy Beat band called The Thamesmen (featuring Ed Begley, Jr. in his Buddy Holly glasses as the nerdy drummer), the band looks at every absurd aspect of the rock music business, from bad album cover designs (the infamous "black album") to backstage food and selling big in Japan. Parodying the destructive demise of drummers like Keith Moon and John Bonham, the band loses drummer after drummer from causes as diverse as "drowning in their own vomit" ("Well, we're not entirely sure it was his *own* vomit. You can't exactly dust for vomit") to spontaneous combustion! The soundtrack from the movie spoofs everything from flower power ("Listen To The Flower People") to rock & roll raunch ("Big Bottom" and "Sex Farm") to the pretentiousness of '70s dinosaur rock ("Stonehenge").

Spinal Tap made an appearance in the "Band Aid" video, heavy metal's contribution to Live Aid. (St. Hubbins declined a solo, because he didn't want to "embarrass" the younger metal singers with his powerful voice.) Spinal Tap did a "reunion" tour in 1992, to capitalize on the nostalgia of their 25th anniversary (just like half the real bands of the '60s and '70s were doing at the time.) They kicked the tour off in Anaheim, California with a hearty "Hello, Cleveland!" and ended up at St. Albert's Hall in London. That concert formed the basis for the follow-up album *Break Like The Wind* (1993) and *A Spinal Tap Reunion,* a rocumentary about what the band had been doing for the past ten years. (For instance, Derek Smalls briefly became a born-again rocker, joined a Christian rock band called Lamb's Blood, and played all the "Monsters of Jesus" festivals!)

All of this is only amusing if you really "get" rock and roll. Younger kids often don't get the joke and tend to believe that Spinal Tap is a real band. Older folks who didn't like or listen to rock music will scratch their heads wondering why everyone is laughing. But for those "in the know," there is no better illustration of how ridiculous the whole business of rock-n-roll can be.

Music Exchange: check out the old Isaac Air Freight/d.a. tune "Sprinkler Head"

STONE TEMPLE PILOTS

Originally called Mighty Joe Young, this grunge rock group from San Diego changed its name to the drug-oriented Stone Temple Pilots (STP was a popular drug in the '60s). Singer Scott Weiland's pink hair and penchant for wearing dresses on stage got them noticed by Atlantic Records. Their first album, *Core* (1992), "is a brooding collection of songs about apathy, oppression, and death that veers from skull-smashing power riffs to soulful ballads" (*Circus,* 3/17/93). Although they give thanks to "God, Jesus Christ" in the album's liner notes, the song "Naked Sunday" makes it clear that they think Christians are hypocritically evil. The song "Sex Type Thing" stirred some controversy, because it was unclear whether it was advocating or mocking macho sexism and date rape. The album sold over 4 million copies. The group has been soundly criticized by the rock press (and some fans) for sounding too much like **Pearl Jam.** They have not taken the criticism well, and their second album *Purple* (1994) moves between the moody self-pity of "Unglued" and "Big Empty" and the angry accusations of "Army Ants."

Violence is not unusual at their concerts. A show on the "Bar-B-Q Mitzvah Tour" with the Butthole Surfers resulted in several broken legs, an attempted rape, and severe injuries when illegal fireworks went off in the crowd (*LAT,* 7/5/93). Frustrated by being pelted with debris by the audience at a concert in Boston, Weiland and his bassist singled out a fan and beat him to a bloody pulp. Sustaining a fractured skull and other injuries, the young man is suing STP for $5 million, but so far the only price they've paid is a free concert in the area and some anti-drug promos (*SDR,* 5/26/94).

The band has also been pretty permissive about sex and drugs. Weiland's sage sexual advice to his fans is: "Try to have as much sex as possible, because it makes for much more peaceful human beings" (*Circus,* 12/30/93). His advice on drugs: "I'm not a champion of drug abuse, but I'm not against experimenting with things" (*RIP,* 5/93). Weiland may be experimenting a bit too much. He was arrested for drug possession in Pasadena after police found heroin, rock cocaine, and a glass pipe for smoking crack in his possession (*APN,* 5/15/95). After the arrest, **Courtney Love** got on the radio and read a statement from him: "I have

131

a disease. It's called drug addiction and I want to say I'm sorry..." (*RS*, 6/29/95). STP has taken a lot of kids for a ride, but the truth is, their advice just doesn't fly. If God isn't the Pilot, this temple's just going to crash and burn.

Music Exchange: Asight Unseen, Grammatrain, Plank Eye, Johnny Q. Public, Sometime Sunday, Yonderboy

T.L.C.

This all-girl hip hop trio from Atlanta is heavy on the seduction tip. Musically, they do a danceable sing-n-rap style called New Jack Swing (or in this case, New Jill Swing, cf **Mary J. Blige**). Their first album, *Ooohhh...on the TLC Tip* (1992), offered the seductive hit "Ain't Too Proud To Beg" (for sex). The second album, *CrazySexyCool* (1994), was even more successful with sexually-charged tunes like "Creep" and "Red Light Special" (with its "Let me be your prostitute" theme.)

This group may understand sex and seduction, but they don't understand love. While Lisa "Left Eye" Lopes was dating football star Andre Rison (Atlantic Falcons), she burned his $1 million house down after an argument (*The Source,* 9/94). The couple showed up to court smiling and holding hands, while Lopes promised not to do it again. She was given five-years probation and a $10,000 fine (*APN,* 1/23/95). The couple planned to marry as soon as she completes a drug and alcohol treatment program and a counseling program for battered women. What are you going to learn about love from these girls? If you want to keep a man, burn his house down? There's got to be a better way to set his heart on fire than this!

Wearing condoms as fashion accessories, they preach "safe" sex and street-level feminism to the dance crowd. This is just another group telling teens, "Forget about AIDS! Forget about sexual diseases! Forget about the epidemic of pregnant teens! Everyone's doing it, so just give in to it! It'll be fine, if you just wear a condom." But as Christian artist Michael Sweet reminds us, there *"ain't no safe way, anymore."* Folks, we've got to learn to dance to a different tune.

Music Exchange: Angie & Debbie (Winans), Out of Eden, YWFC

2 LIVE CREW

Luther Campbell brought X-rated party rap into the mainstream with this controversial crew from Florida. Their first album, *2 Live Crew Is What We Are* (1986), set the pattern with its obscene, sexual fantasies. They started to receive national attention with the release of *As Nasty As They Wanna Be* in 1989. That album contains 226 uses of the "F" word alone—along with 117 explicit terms for male or female genitalia, 87 descriptions of oral sex, and over a dozen illustrations of violent sex. A sample of Homeboy Condoms were included in the album, as if they were promoting safe sex. There was a cleaned-up version for radio airplay called *As Clean As They Wanna Be*, but it didn't help. The album was declared pornographic in several counties in Florida, and people were arrested for selling the album to minors (*BB*, 3/10/90)—an act considered unjust by those who felt it was 2 Live Crew who should have been arrested instead. (They were later tried for obscenity, but the jury failed to convict them.)

Banned In The USA (1990) (as in Bruce Springsteen's *Born In The USA*) included more obscenities and some half-baked rhetoric about censorship. They produced a collection of videos to accent these ideas, but the video's producer was not won over by their message. Penelope Spheeris, who is best known for her rock music documentaries *The Decline of Western Civilization, Part One* (about punk) and *Part Two* (about heavy metal), was appalled by their material: "You hear about the lyrics, but you don't imagine they'd be anywhere near as offensive as they are. They couldn't get much worse, except in a snuff movie. I was pretty shocked," she confessed. "This project caused me to define my own values. Two years ago, I didn't believe in record stickering. Now I do" (*USA*, 8/22/90).

Subsequent albums have not sold well. Trying to stay on top, they have only grown more pornographic. During concerts in Japan, they went beyond simulated sex, and were caught on camera actually doing the dirty deed on stage with their "dancing" girls (*USA*, 8/23/94). Despite these extremes, "their brand of X-rated humor seems almost tame compared to the mix of explicit sex and violence available on more hardcore gansta rap sessions, while Jamaican toasters like Shabba Ranks and the Mad Cobra [reggae musicians] outdistanced them in creative lewdness" (*AMG*, pg. 657). But don't buy into the argument that they're okay now because they're not as bad as some rap groups. Christians should be comparing this crew to God's best, not to the world's worst. Minds exposed to this rap won't be as clean as they wanna be until they're washed in the Word of Christ (Rom. 12:1-2).

Music Exchange: Disciples of Christ, Dynamic Twins, Freedom of Soul

TOOL

This hardcore ensemble formed in Hollywood in 1988. Both their EP (*Opiate*, 1992) and their LP (*Undertow*, 1993) are filled with lyrics that "explore the darkest, most disturbing aspects of human behavior" (*BAM*, 11/5/93). They vilify religion in songs like "Opiate" and "Sober" and offer a twisted tale of sodomy in "Prison Sex." Songs like "Hush" and "Jerk-Off" (*"It doesn't matter what's right / It's only wrong if you get caught / I should play God and just shoot you myself"*) are angry expressions of self-justified anarchy. "Tool's view of humanity is grim, to say the least. Ask [singer] Maynard Keenan if he hates people and he responds, 'Pretty much, I'd have to say absolutely.' Why? 'Ignorance,' he says" (*BAM*, 11/5/93).

> "If and when I ever overcome my fear of death, I will surely die by my own hand. If I get to the point where I become a burden, then I will have the decency to kill myself."
> - Peter Steele of Type-O-Negative

Tool ascribes to a perverse bit of psycho-babble known as "lachrymology" (the study of crying), which is supposed to help them channel their pain away from self-destruction to something positive. But nothing positive is being fashioned by this Tool. Their music is simply a bitter form of primal screaming that feeds their unrestrained anger. Subjecting your mind to the constant hammering of Tool's hatred of humanity is nothing less than a form of self-abuse.

Music Exchange: Everdown, Wish for Eden

Shania TWAIN

While this 29-year-old Canadian beauty finds herself at the top of the country music charts, she is not a typical country star. "She doesn't live anywhere near Nashville, and not once in a five-hour interview did she thank God for her success. She doesn't even eat meat, for pete's sake!" (*EW*, 8/11/95). Shania (pronounced Shuh-NYE-uh—it's an Ojibwa Indian word for "I'm on my way") attributes her new success to her husband, British record producer John "Mutt" Lange, who is more famous for working with arena rock acts like **AC/DC,** Def Leppard, **Michael Bolton,** and Bryan Adams than with country acts. Her album *The Woman In Me* has yeilded hits like "Who's Bed Have Your Boots Been Under?" and "Any Man of Mine." Her tunes are typical tales of heading-for-the-bar-'cause-you-keep-cheatin'-on-me, without offering much hope of anything changing. She may be easy on the ears and eyes, but her world of human heartaches is one without the healing hand of God.

Music Exchange: Andi Landis, Susie Luchsinger

TUPAC

Originally part of the rap group Digital Underground, Tupac Shakur has gone on to a successful solo and movie career. He starred in *Poetic Justice* with Janet Jackson, and had a role in *Menace II Society*, but was fired by director John Hughes. He later went after Mr. Hughes, brandishing a loaded weapon and threatening to kill him. Despite this, he was later offered several other movie roles.

Tupac's rising success was accompanied by a series of criminally self-destructive acts. Eventually he developed a "rap sheet" longer than a stretch limousine. His string of accusations and arrests include: 1) an arrest in Los Angeles for assaulting a limo driver who dared suggest that he not do drugs in the limo; 2) a warrant out for his arrest for an assault-and-battery charge in an incident where he was accused of slapping a woman who had the audacity to ask for his autograph; 3) charges stemming from a shoot-out with two off-duty policemen in Atlanta (his defence was that he didn't realize they were policemen); 4) an arrest for his part in aiding two men to sodomize a 20-year-old female fan in a New York City hotel room. This last charge ultimately came to trial, where he was declared guilty and sentenced to 4 1/2 years in prison.

While Tupac virtually defined gansta rap (he called it "Thug Life"), now that he's actually in jail, he's begun to change his tune. In an interview from behind bars, Shakur denounced his criminal lifestyle. "Thug Life to me is dead. If it's real, let somebody else represent it, because I'm tired of it. I represented it too much. I was Thug Life." (*VIBE*, 4/95). This belated repentance may not make the gansta life any less glamorous to kids, however. "The whole prison-poet thing is very cool to kids. These type of rappers are deified by the kids; they're like modern superheroes," claims his record company (*EW*, 12/16/94). Nor will it affect Tupac's profit margin. Even while in jail, he had a new album and a movie (*Bullet*) released as he began his prison sentence. Some may call it unfair and some may call it Poetic Justice. Rest assured, in the end, justice will be served.

"Do not associate with a man given to anger; or go with a hot-tempered man, lest you learn his ways, and find a snare for yourself " (Prov. 22:24-25, NAS).

Music Exchange: Gospel Ganstas, King Shon & the S.S. M.O.B, T-Bone

TYPE-O-NEGATIVE
....

Originally called Carnivore, this Brooklyn-based band started out as a typical thrash outfit in 1983. They offended almost everyone with racist ("Race War") and sexist ("Male Supremacy") messages on their albums (*Carnivore* and *Retaliation*). The band broke up in 1988, and singer Peter Steele went back to driving a garbage truck. Depressed and suicidal, Steele formed T-O-N in 1990, and released the album *Slow, Deep and Hard* in 1991. "The whole thing was written in one drunk, feeling-sorry-for-myself Friday night," confessed Steele (*APN*, 3/95). The album continued Carnivore's legacy: a song called "Der Untermensch" was so racist, they canceled part of their European tour because posters appeared in Germany declaring "Kill this band on sight" (*BB*, 1/18/92).

On *Bloody Kisses* (1993), they moved to a style they call gothadelic industrimetal: a confused combination of **Black Sabbath**'s sludge metal, hardcore rhythms, gothic keyboards, and morosely aching melodies. It would make an ideal soundtrack for a horror movie: "So evil sounding is it that if the Prince of Darkness ever cut an album, this is undoubtedly how he would sound" (*RS*, 2/23/95). The lyrics are full of pain, betrayal, and disillusionment. "Christian Woman" blames religion (especially the Catholic church) for all the sexual repression and guilt that goes on in society. "Suspended in Dusk" and "Black No. 1" romanticizes vampirism and the gothic lifestyle. "Girls ask to suck my blood. I can show you scars all over me where I've taken razor blades and opened myself up and let them stick their tongues into me" (*AP*, 3/95)

Fans see them as darkly romantic, but the real message here is destruction. "Mankind is destined for self-destruction," says Steele, "which will be a definite improvement. When the human race is off the planet, it will be better for nature" (*MM*, 4/95). Steele's apparent hatred of humanity is just a cover for his own self-loathing. "He calls himself 'a monster,' 'a psychopath,' 'a social retard.' But what he seems to be is sensitive, wary, and almost paralyzed by low self-esteem" (*APN*, 12/14/94). Songs like "Gravitational Constant" and "Bloody Kisses" advocate suicide as a legitimate option. "If and when I ever overcome my fear of death, I will surely die by my own hand. If I get to the point where I become a burden, then I will have the decency to kill myself" (*RIP*, 11/91). It's tragic to be losing so many young people to those who lie in a pagan haze. The solution does not lie in the destruction of humanity, but in the healing of the heart by Jesus Christ.

Music Exchange: No Laughing Matter, Savior Machine

U2

Originally an obscure Irish pub band, they ultimately became the band of the 1980s. They formed in 1976, when the five lads were still in school. (Fifth wheel, Dick Evans, left to form a punk band called The Virgin Prunes). Vocalist Paul Hewson (renaming himself Bono Vox after seeing a billboard ad for hearing aids) was the son of a Protestant mother (who died when he was 14) and a Catholic father (in Ireland, they are at war over such things.) Guitarist The Edge (Dave Evans) developed a unique guitar sound that was copied by dozens of bands on both sides of the Atlantic. Larry Mullen (drums) and Adam Clayton (bass) round out the group. Their three-song EP (*U2:3*, 1979), topped the charts in Ireland, but nowhere else (U2 played one of its first English gigs to 9 people).

Signed to Island Records, the first two albums did not fare all that well outside of Ireland. *Boy* (1980) was rough but energetic. *October* (1981) was tinged with Christian imagery, especially in songs like "Gloria" and "Rejoice." *War* (1983) became their breakthrough album and set the tenor for the band's image. "Sunday Bloody Sunday" is an impassioned commentary on the bombings in Belfast and the social unrest in Ireland. The album is full of anguish and protest, yet it closes on an optimistic note, "40," a musical rendition of Psalm 40 ("*I will sing a new song*"). *Under a Blood Red Sky* (1983) captured their concert at Red Rocks in Colorado. *The Unforgettable Fire* (1984) has almost become their forgotten album, although it contains "Pride In the Name of Love," dedicated to Martin Luther King, Jr.

U2 hit their peak in 1987 with *Joshua Tree*. They struck a chord around the world with their social/political idealism and their cautious optimism. They became deeply involved with Band Aid and Live Aid, raising money for the famine in Africa (Bono and the Edge are said to have chartered their own plane and personally distributed food to the needy, away from the public eye.) They were part of the anti-apartheid project *Sun City* and Amnesty International's *Conspiracy of Hope* tour. They were also more than a little open about their Christianity.

As their impassioned idealism put them on a pedestal as some kind of Musical Messiahs, cynical rock critics turned on them, suddenly finding them preachy and pretentious. *Rattle and Hum* (1988) was soundly criticized as ego-centric and self-serving. *Achtung Baby* (1991) was a dark change of pace, as U2 seemed to be taking the criticism to heart, losing their idealistic edge. Their Zoo TV tour blew up the observations of "Bullet, The Blue Sky" into a multi-media extravaganza. A bleak and bitter blast at the corruption and decadence of our lives, it pulled in over 2 million fans and resulted in the *Zooropa* album (1993).

Christians have been on both sides of the fence about U2. Critics often cited their song "I Still Haven't Found What I'm Looking For" as evidence that they were lost. That criticism ignored convicting lyrics that they were simply looking for a living enactment of the Kingdom of God on earth. In those days, U2 was one of the few secular bands that I would recommend to church kids. In a concert review I co-authored in 1987, I praised them as "simple and unpretentious performers" with "the uncanny ability to be godly without being gaudy." Bono seemed to shine with a genuine vulnerability that allowed him to "envelope 15,000 fans in a warm, hopeful embrace" (*CCM*, 6/87).

But those days changed somewhere along the line. Perhaps they grew weary of a world that never seemed to change despite their powerful pleas. Perhaps they were too vulnerable to the vicious attacks of their critics. The music industry is full of bitter cynics who will blast anyone who dares to present the hopeful notion that there is a way out of their dark gutter of despair. As these critical missiles found their mark, U2 seems to have found a harshly bitter perspective of their own, reflected in their current work: "U2 seems to be caught in a bitter dialectic of spiritual searching and artistic ambition. Their dark, cynical worldview has hamstrung the appeal of their album (*Zooropa*)" (*World*, 7/31/93).

What is most disheartening is that they have lost their faithful focus, centering on the hypocritical antics of American evangelists, as if they were the only reflection of religion in the world today. Failing to find what they were looking for, they seem to have given up the search. It is a sober reminder of what comes from failing to follow the principles of Scripture: "If then you have been raised up with Christ, keep seeking the things above, where Christ is, seated at the right hand of God. Set your mind on [be intent on] the things above, not on the things that are on earth" (Col. 3:1-2, NAS). I, for one, sincerely hope that U2 will look up again and recapture their Unforgettable Fire.

Music Exchange: the Choir, Curious Fools, Love Coma, the 77's, Vector

VAN HALEN

Yes, the name does mean "from hell" (in Dutch), but it is Eddie and Alex Van Halen's real last name. Their father was a Dutch jazz musician, who moved to America when the boys were in their early teens. Joining Michael Anthony (with his Jack Daniels bottle-shaped bass) and David Lee Roth (vocals), Eddie (guitar) and Alex (drums) formed phase one of Van Halen in Pasedena, California in 1974. Heard while playing at club by **KISS**'s Gene Simmons, they soon signed a record contract. Eddie's lightning fast guitar work and unique tapping style, along with David Lee's flamboyant frontman routines made them one of the most popular party metal bands in America. Their first release, *Van Halen* (1978), went platinum, as has every record they've released since. Roth used to introduce a song from that album, "Running with the Devil," by saying "Not even God can save your soul at a Van Halen concert!" Upon hearing this arrogant claim at a concert in 1980, one young man immediately prayed to receive Christ, and he's been evangelizing ever since (*RS*, 6/19/87). They hit the peak of their popularity with hits like "Jump" and "Hot for Teacher" on their album *1984*.

David Lee Roth quit in 1985 and started a solo career, which started off strongly with hit albums like *Crazy From the Heat* (1985) (with its successful cover of the Beach Boys' "California Girls"), *Eat 'Em & Smile* (1986) and *Skyscraper* (1988) [with Steve Vai (guitar) and Billy Sheehan (on bass)]. Subsequent efforts (1991's *A Little Ain't Enough* and 1994's *Your Filthy Little Mouth*) were less successful, and Roth has basically faded away with the glam metal scene itself.

Van Halen continued on with phase two of the band, sometimes jokingly referred to as Van Hagar. Sammy Hagar, the former singer with the almost-popular rock band Montrose, proved to be a more-than-adequate replacement for Roth. His first album with the band *5150* (a police code for mentally unstable) became the band's first #1 album on the charts. The follow-up albums also charted well: *OU812* (1988) (sound out each number and letter to get the crude joke) and *For Unlawful Carnal Knowledge*

> "**N**ot even God can save your soul at a Van Halen concert!"
> - David Lee Roth of Van Halen

(1991) (the first letter of each words spells out a word that would not be found on the album cover otherwise). The album *Balance* (1995) brought some controversy over its distasteful cover photo of naked Siamese Twins sitting on a see-saw, especially in Japan where such things are not considered amusing since we dropped the bomb (*AP*, 2/61/95). Eddie married TV sweetheart Valerie Bertinelli and they had a boy, whom they saddled with the unfortunate moniker of Wolfgang Van Halen.

Like **Aerosmith** and the Rolling Stones, Van Halen has basically become a bunch of 40-year-old men trying to hustle 16-year-old girls with their music. Eddie's guitar style was once brilliant in its speed and execution, but younger guitarists have copied and bettered him since then. Eddie's bouts with alcohol almost killed his carreer, his marriage, and his ability to play, although he claims to be staying sober these days. Van Halen's party mentality and crude sexual tease seems silly and superficial in light of the heavy nihilism of today's grunge, industrial, alternative, and hardcore styles. Roth may have believed that no one could get saved at a Van Halen concert, but the truth is they couldn't save themselves. Instead of running with the Devil, fans ought to be running the race for Christ instead (1 Cor. 9:24; Heb. 12:1-2; 2 Tim. 4:7).

Music Exchange: Guardian, Halo, Holy Soldier, Lex Rex, Shout/Tamplin, Whitecross

Suzanne VEGA
....

Suzanne Vega re-opened the doors for folk music while the rest of the country was going ga-ga over glam metal in the late '80s. She was inspired by the likes of Woody Guthrie, Bob Dylan, and Joni Mitchell, to whom she is often compared. The song "Luka," her portrayal of child abuse, was one of the first top 40 songs to broach this sensitive topic. Like her counterpart, Janis Ian, Vega paints dark portraits of loneliness, rejection, solitude, fear and quiet determination. Her lyrics are somewhat bleak and depressing, but they are not filled with the self-indulgent pity of Morrissey or the hopeless despair of **The Cure.**

She offers observations without obligations—understanding rather than resignation. Her sensitive insights can be helpful to the Christian looking to overcome the temptations of assembly-line salvation. But it is not quite music to believe in. There are no answers here, only observations, which are colored by her own spiritual orientation (she is a practicing Buddhist). This music will not help you focus on things above (Col. 3:2). But for those who work in the church, there are valuable reminders here about the pain of loneliness and the peace of solitude that people are experiencing in this life.

Music Exchange: Carolyn Arends, Bob Bennett, Nicola Gianconia, Pam Mark Hall, Kim Hill, Jan Krist, Grover Levy, Derek Lind, Riki Michelle, Out of the Gray, Serena & Pearl

WEEN

Dean and Gene Ween are what you would get if Beavis and Butthead had been raised on college radio instead of heavy metal. Mickey Melchiondo and Aaron Freeman first met in 1983 when they were 14 years old. They started putting their gross junior high humor to music, when they were in, well, junior high. They became Dean and Gene Ween and haven't grown up a bit since. Albums like *Pure Guava* (1992) are full of vulgarities, mocking everyone and everything in their path: cruelty to animals ("Squish the Weasel"), dying pets ("Mister, Would You Please Help My Pony?"), and victims of disease ("Spinal Meningitis Got Me Down" and "The HIV Song"). Rumors of constant drug use and a story about being possessed during an experiment with the occult only add to the outrageous image. There's nothing for Christians here. These guys are even too gross for the **Green Jelly** crowd.

Music Exchange: Breakfast with Amy, Danielson, Fluffy, Lust Control, MxPx, One Bad Pig

WEEZER

Weezer found fame and fortune right out of the box with their debut album (1994) and a little hit ditty called "Undone (the Sweater Song)," about the risk of being vulnerable in a relationship. Their music could be described as **Beach Boys** meets **Green Day.** Their update of the Beach Boys' "I Get Around," and "In My Room" comes through as "In My Garage": *"I've got posters on the wall / Of my favorite rock group KISS / I've got Ace Frehley, I've got Peter Criss / Waiting there for me"* (*CDH*, 3/23/95). They have the goofy spontaneity and pop/punk accessibility which makes them as appealing to 10-year-old boys and junior high girls, as to

143

the pseudo-sophisticated college radio set.

Although the band formed in L.A., all the members are transplants from the East Coast. The key figure is singer/songwriter Rivers Cuomo, who claims to have been raised in the sheltered environment of a Hindu community in Connecticut called Yogaville. Like J. Mascis of Dinosaur Jr., he is painfully shy and constantly self-critical. "The World Has Turned and Left Me Here" is probably the best reflection of the album's theme: feeling lost and left behind in a big world. While this group seems fun and playful, the heart of their music reveals a lonely little orphan who can't find his way home. While we all may feel that way from time to time, we'll never come Undone if we remember that our Father has a mansion for the orphans He's adopted (Jn. 14:2). And He's waiting to show us the way Home.

Music Exchange: Clash of Symbols, Dell Griffiths, Jars of Clay, Eugene Levy, Plank Eye, Villanelle, Walter Eugenes

WHITE ZOMBIE
••

This industrial noise/metal band has taken a comic book mentality to mixing horror movies and schlock pop culture to create one of the more popular rock monsters of the mid-90s. The mad scientist behind this rock-n-roll Frankenstein is Rob Straker, alias Rob Zombie, who was once a production assistant on the TV show "Pee Wee's Playhouse." Zombie sings, does all the art for the T-shirts and CD's, and produces most of the bizarre noises on their albums. The group formed in 1985 in New York when Zombie met Sean Yseult (bassist) at art school. They named their band after the Bela Lugosi's 1932 horror classic. Their look is reminiscent of another pop/metal joke called Zodiac Mindwarp who never found this much acceptance.

Zombie's early creations (*Soul Crusher,* 1987; *Make Them Die Slowly,* 1989) didn't get off the table. Their third monstrosity, *La Sexorcisto: Devil Music, Vol. 1* (1992), almost didn't come to life either. Almost a year after its release, it had only sold 75,000 copies. But when Beavis and Butthead saw the video for the single, "Thunder Kiss '65" and pronounced it "cool" (heh-heh, heh-heh), suddenly it was a hit. The album sold 300,000 copies in less than six weeks, and ultimately went platinum. "Beavis and Butthead are the Siskel and Ebert of the retarded generation," says Zombie, "but I guess kids really do care what they say" (*EW,* 10/8/93). Who says MTV doesn't affect anyone? Not that the album is anything you want to bury yourself in. "It's an electric funeral, a morbid mantra of sex, cars, tattoos, guns, sex, death—all the good stuff—spewed out like Linda Blair's projectile vomit" (*RIP,* 7/93).

The next album, called *Astro-Creep: 2000 (Songs of Love, Destruction, and Other Synthetic Delusions of the Electric Head)* (1995), shot up into *Billboard's* Top 10 and went platinum in a matter of weeks. The album is more pop-culture in a blender, full of bizarre noise, pseudo-Satanism, and sonic overkill. But don't be fooled by the obvious. They aren't really out to turn your kids into sex-crazed Satanists. They want to bait parents and straight-laced, middle-class Americans into reacting to this ridiculous torrent of pop/schlock insanity. When the 700 Club branded them the new leaders of Satanism in rock, it played right into their hands. That's exactly what they want us to think. Perhaps, the best way to respond to their manipulative ploy is to treat it as the impotent joke it is, and don't buy into any of it. Come to think of it, that's usually a good way to deal with the Devil himself.

Music Exchange: Circle of Dust, Mortal, Precious Death, Tourniquet

"Weird Al" YANKOVIC

Alfred Yankovic was born in California in 1960 and started accordion lessons at the age of 7. "It was lucky that my parents had the foresight to realize that accordions would dominate rock and roll, because that put me in the forefront of today's big accordion movement!" (*Happening,* 9/87). He started using the name Weird Al during his years as a college radio DJ. In 1979 he started getting attention with "My Bologna" (a take on the Knack's "My Sharona"), recorded in a bathroom at his college. "Another One Rides the Bus" (a take on Queen's "Another One Bites the Dust") was recorded live on Dr. Demento's show with Al (on accordion, of course) and his drummer, Bermuda Schwartz(!). It became Dr. Demento's most requested single ever. "I guess you could call him my De-*mentor.* I really owe it all to him" (*People,* 4/16/84). "Ricky" (based on Toni Basil's "Mickey") and "I Love Rocky Road" (a spoof of Joan Jett's "I Love Rock and Roll") followed.

It was Weird Al's parody of **Michael Jackson,** the King of Pop, that ultimately made him the King of Pop Parody! The single "Eat It" went gold and actually ate its way up the charts faster than the song it parodied (Jackson's "Beat It"). He also spoofed Jackson's hit "I'm Bad" with a tune called "I'm Fat" (1988). *Dare To Be Stupid* (1985) included "Like A Surgeon" (a take on **Madonna's** "Like a Virgin"). *Off The Deep End* (1992) featured a sendup of **Nirvana's** hit "Smells Like Teen Spirit," which capped on Kurt Cobain's singing style: *"Sing distinctly? / We don't wanna / Buy our album / We're Nirvana."* After years of pop music success, Weird Al has accomplished all he ever dreamed of: "My ultimate goal is to be bigger than the Partridge Family" (*People,* 4/16/84).

Adults often find Yankovic pretty silly, but many kids find him hilari-ous. Yankovic's humor is generally clean. He maintains a healthy disdain of pop music idol worship. No one is too sacred to spoof, and yet his par-odies of pop culture are never mean-spirited or vindictive. This attitude helps keep kids in check who might tend to take their music too seriously. The worst that can be said is that this is Twinkie music—tasty tidbits of humor devoid of any spiritual food value. This is an apt analogy since Weird Al, like the junior high boys that are his biggest fans, is obsessed with food. Dads who can appreciate Weird Al's sense of humor just might find they have something in common with their adolescent sons after all. As they can listen to these zany songs together, dads can recapture some of their own silly youth, while building a bridge to their sons.

Music Exchange: Paul Aldrich, Larry Bubb, Mark Lowry, Randy Stonehill, Swirling Eddies

ZZ TOP

....

This bearded, boogie blues-rock trio formed in Houston, Texas in 1970, and once called themselves the Warlocks. Some suggest their name is a homage to B.B. King. However, it's usually said to be a reference to two popular brands of rolling papers used to roll (marijuana) cigarettes: Zig Zag and Top. Their first hit was "LaGrange" (an ode to a whorehouse) from the album *Tres Hombres* (1973).

> "*My* ultimate goal is to be bigger than the Partridge Family."
> - *Weird Al Yankovic*

Their Worldwide Texas Tour in 1976 featured a Texas-shaped stage with live buffalo, steer, and real rattlesnakes. It lasted 18 months and made over $10 million, becoming one of the largest-grossing concert tours in rock history. Exhausted from the tour, the band took a 2 1/2 year vacation. They came back in 1979 with their trademark beards (except for drummer Frank Beard, who was clean shaven). The *Eliminator* album (1983), followed by *Afterburner* (1985), brought them into the world of MTV with sexually provocative videos for songs like "Legs," "Sharp Dressed Man," and "Velcro Fly." By 1986 they were once again the #1 concert draw in the country.

In 1985, bassist Dusty Hill accidentally shot himself when his loaded Derringer fell out of his boot. He recovered. In 1987, they petitioned NASA to be the first rock-n-roll band to play in space. When they were turned down, they booked advance passage to be on the first public flight to the moon. They were relatively inactive in the late 1980s, but in 1992 they signed a $40 million dollar contract with Sony. In 1994, they released *Antenna* with more sexual-tease tunes like "Fuzzbox Voodoo" and "Girl in a T-Shirt." After 25 years, they are the only band in rock music history still playing with all its original members.

ZZ Top's reputation as hell-raising, beer-drinking good-old-boys gives them a gritty appeal to the blue-collar, working-class crowd. Their idea of a good time always involves fast cars and faster girls, making them the ultimate booze, babes, and beards band. Unlike the crude bands of today, they cover their sexual fantasies in clever innuendo with songs like "Dust My Broom," "Cover My Rig," or "Pearl Necklace." They're the kind of band the church used to ignore because there's nothing obviously occultic about them. This band isn't about Satan, it's about sex. Their talent lies solely in keeping grown-up men lost in junior high fantasies. But ZZ Top's "Legs" won't help you walk in the Kingdom.

Music Exchange: Greg Chaisson, DeGarmo & Key

APPENDICES

WHY THEY LISTEN

Looking at today's secular music can leave Christian parents pretty puzzled. Why would perfectly decent Christian kids want to listen to so much indecent music? It's important not to take a simplistic approach toward rock music and teens. The music can be boiled down to black and white, good and evil. But helping kids grow into strong Christian adults cannot. What's most important here is not how evil the music may or may not be. What's important is *learning why* your children choose this music. After twenty-five years of working with kids in the church and on the streets, I find that there are usually three basic reasons:

1) They listen to it because their friends do. Teens are not initially concerned with the themes and deeper spiritual questions of the music. They just want to belong and fit in with their friends. Rather than simply trying to isolate and alienate your kids from their friends, you can use the music as a springboard for talking about courage, standing up for what you believe, and facing peer pressure.

2) There are ideas in the music that teens honestly relate to, especially on the emotional level. Many teens feel awkward, ugly, overwhelmed, and unprepared for the future. Most alternative music today describes those feelings very well. Instead of simply reacting to the style of the music, you can use the music as a springboard to talk about the doubts and fears that teens have about growing up.

3) Sometimes the music is simply a symbol of their independence. Teens want to be independent human beings, not just clones of their parents. Music is often a way of trying to find something that's uniquely "their own"—something their parents did not pick for them. It's their way of saying, "Look, I'm my own person." In trying to do this, they may make some foolish choices that will frustrate you, but it is not the same as angry, defiant rebellion. Instead of berating a 15-year-old for not making 40-year-old choices, you can use the music as a springboard to discuss what it means to be an individual yielded to Christ.

Communicating with your children about their music does not have to end up in some epic battle. Understanding these motivations can help you talk to your teens better without over-reacting. Remember, the goal here isn't simply to remove the music you loathe. It's to draw your kids closer to Jesus Christ—and you.

THE FOUR PHILOSOPHIES OF ROCK MUSIC

One of the scriptural foundations that Al Menconi Ministries is based on is Colossians 2:8 (LB): "Don't let others spoil your faith and joy with their **philosophies**, their wrong and shallow answers built on men's thoughts and ideas, instead of on what Christ has said" (emphasis mine). In other words, it's important to look at the message in the music to determine whether it's suitable for a godly life. Just what *are* some of the messages in today's music that could spoil the joy of our salvation and our faith in Christ? I believe there are at least four basic messages or philosophies that are being preached in today's music:

Hedonism

This is the philosophy that says, "Eat, drink, and be merry—for tomorrow, we die." It says, "Live for today, and don't worry about tomorrow." "If it feels good—do it!" It focuses on enjoying the present in order to forget about the past and ignore the future. It is very materialistic, here and now, and self-centered. It's summed up by that bumper sticker that says: "He who dies with the most toys wins!" (Actually, he who dies with the most toys, still dies.) The gospel of hedonism preaches that we find our freedom by following our feelings.

Hedonism does away with consequences and responsibilities. It either ignores them altogether—"Do what you want. There's no price to pay!" Or it excuses crazy behaviors by saying, "Hey, we're all going to die sooner or later, anyway!" You won't find a better example than in Prince's song "1999." In that song he said that we're all going to die in the year 2000, so we might as well party like it's 1999. In other words, the solution to our destruction is to ignore our problems and dance our lives away.

You'll find this philosophy in party rock and glam metal, like **Van Halen** and Bon Jovi. It is also found in the careless romance of pop/dance music from **Madonna** to **En Vogue**, and in the R&B and light rap of **R. Kelly** or **Salt-N-Pepa.** You'll even find it in country music. The problem with this philosophy is simple. It flatly contradicts what Jesus teaches. Jesus clearly says that we must deny ourselves and follow Him (Mt.

154

16:24-26). Every weekend teens are faced with temptations about sex and drugs and things that promise them freedom. The music teaches them to give in and go for it. But as Leslie Phillips sang, "You can live for the weekend, but only Jesus can take you beyond Saturday night."

Nihilism

This term comes from the Latin (*nihil*) which means "nothing" (as in the word *annihilate*—destroying something until there's nothing left). The philosophy of nihilism is that life is empty and meaningless. It's a wasted effort. Since there is no rhyme or reason to life, and there is nothing after death, nothing matters. What's the use? Why try? It's like that bumper sticker that says, "Life's a bummer, then you die." The real bummer is that so many kids accept this idea. They see life as one mindless march into the cold, heartless machine of life, to be used up until you die. No one cares, nothing matters, everything is an empty effort. Pretty depressing, huh?

These ideas were fostered by the French existentialists Jean Paul Sartre and Albert Camus whose works were published in the 1940s and 1950s. Their works suffered a resurgence of popularity on the college campuses in the late 1960s. Also influential are the depressing lives and works of Anne Sexton and Sylvia Plath. (By the way, these authors are required reading in many public schools today.) Musically kids are getting this message in grunge metal, industrial rock, goth music, and much of what is being called alternative music today. Some of the chief preachers of this dark gospel are Morrissey, **Nirvana,** and **Nine Inch Nails.**

Jesus did not teach these themes. He did not teach us to embrace death: "I am come that they might have *LIFE,* and have it more abundantly" (Jn 10:10, KJV, emphasis mine). He did not suggest that our efforts are empty: "In this world you will have trouble. But take heart! I have overcome the world" (Jn. 16:33, NIV). He did not teach that life is nothing but a hopeless struggle. He *is* our Hope. "This I recall to my mind, and therefore I have hope...the Lord is my portion, saith my soul, therefore I will hope in Him. It is good that a man should both hope and quietly wait for the salvation of the Lord" (Lam. 3:21, 24, 26, KJV).

Absurdism

If life is meaningless, you can respond in one of two ways: you can give in to despair or you can laugh in its face. Nihilism reflects the first choice, and Absurdism marks the second. Like the nihilist, the absurdist believes that life is pretty pointless. But rather than responding in a passive retreat, the absurdist puts his energy into mocking life. Since life is ridiculous, why not ridicule everything? The only way to deal with a meaningless universe is to treat it like one big cosmic joke. Absurdists are actually pretty angry and express themselves through cynicism, sarcasm, and facetious tongue-in-cheek humor.

With absurdists, the world as we know it is upside down. You can't rely on "normal" interpretations with this music. Some songs are so violent and sexual, it's absurd. For example, Suicidal Tendencies has a song called "I Saw Your Mommy, and Your Mommy Was Dead!" Some of the lyrics go: *"I saw your mommy and your mommy was dead / I saw her lying in a pool of red / Chewed off toes next to her chopped off feet / I took a picture 'cause I thought it was neat."* Absurdists see this as a funny joke. Bands like **Anthrax,** the Beastie Boys, and the Red Hot Chili Peppers are seen as a sort of Three Stooges of thrash. Some groups could be said to be absurd because they clearly have nothing to say. Their lyrics are undecipherable, even when written out in front of you. These ideas are designed to appeal to a junior high sense of humor. Bands like **Green Jelly, Gwar,** and Primus perform in ways that are crude, silly, and downright stupid—and they are proud of it!

The Bible refers to these people as scoffers, mockers, and fools: "First of all, you must understand that in the last days scoffers will come, scoffing and following their own evil desires (2 Pet. 3:3, NIV). "The proud and arrogant man—'Mocker' is his name; he behaves with over*ween*ing pride" (Prov. 21:24, NIV). [Actually, **Ween** is a great example of this principle.] "A fool finds no pleasure in understanding, but delights in airing his own opinions" (Prov. 18:2, NIV). God does not promise a great future for such people: "He mocks proud mockers, but gives grace to the humble" (Prov. 3:34, NIV); "The ruthless will vanish, the mockers will disappear, and all who have an eye for evil will be cut down..." (Isa. 29:20, NIV); "Penalties are prepared for mockers, and beatings for the backs of fools" (Prov. 19:29, NIV). The Bible offers this advise to those who are entertained by the mocker: "Drive out the mocker, and out goes strife; quarrels and insults are ended" (Prov. 22:10, NIV) and "The way of the fool seems right to him, but a wise man listens to advice" (Prov. 12:15, NIV).

Rebellion
....

For the purposes of this book, the philosophy of rebellion refers to an open anger—a rage at the world and what life has to offer. This is the music that curses God, defies authority, and shakes its fist at the world. If you've been thinking about the first three philosophies, you might be inclined to ask: "Aren't all these philosophies rebellious?" Well yes, they are. They are all in rebellion to God's Word. But they all express a different attitude in that rebellion. The *hedonist* avoids life's problems by partying. The *nihilist* believes that life is pointless and gives up. The *absur-*

dist believes that life is ridiculous and mocks life for being so stupid. The *rebellious* want to take life by the throat and beat it senseless. Do you see the difference?

Punk music made anger an art-form in the late '70s. Heavy metal took up the banner in the '80s, especially with the advent of speed and thrash metal groups like Megadeth and **Metallica**. In the '90s, this angry metal took the form of death metal and grindcore. You can usually identify these groups, when they go by names like Death, Obituary, or **Cannibal Corpse.** Some of these bands, like **Deicide** and **Morbid Angel,** go beyond death and dismemberment into actual Satanism. This angry rebellion is also found in the hard hip-hop and street rap styles known as gansta rap or hardcore rap. Songs like **Ice-T's** "Cop Killer" and **Ice Cube's** "Death Certificate" are a dead giveaway.

Obviously, this is not what Jesus teaches. The Bible says that rebellion against God is just as bad as the sin of witchcraft or Satanism (1 Sam. 15:23). And God is pretty clear how we should respond to people who teach the anger and violence of rebellion: "Do not be envious of evil men, nor desire to be with them, for their minds devise violence, and their lips talk of trouble" (Prov. 24:1-2, NAS); "Do not associate with a man given to anger, or go with a hot-tempered man, lest you learn his ways and find a snare for yourself" (Prov. 22:24-25, NAS).

Understanding these philosophies can really help you improve your communication with your kids when talking about rock and rap. You'll just end up going around and around with your kids if you focus on rumors and speculations like backmasking and the "demon beat." But if you ask the right questions, you'll find yourself having deeper and more constructive conversations with them. In practical terms, Colossians 2:8 is suggesting three simple questions to ask your children (and yourself!): 1) "What are your favorite music groups teaching?" 2) "Is that what Jesus would teach?" and 3) "How is your faith in Christ and the joy of your salvation today?"

BIBLIOGRAPHY

Erlewine, Michael (with Chris Woodstra and Vladimir Bogdanov), edit. *All Music Guide.* San Francisco: Miller Freeman Books, 1994.

Heatley, Michael, edit. *The Ultimate Encyclopedia of Rock.* New York: Harper-Collins, 1993.

Lazell, Barry (with Dafydd Rees and Luke Crampton), edit. *Rock Movers and Shakers.* New York: Billboard Publications, 1989.

Menconi, Al (with Dave Hart). *Today's Music: A Window To Your Child's Soul.* Elgin, Illinois: David C. Cook Publishers, 1990.

Pareles, Jon and Romanowski, Patricia, edit. *The Rolling Stone Encyclopedia of Rock-n-Roll.* New York: Summit Books, 1983.

Seay, Davin (with Mary Neely). *Stairway to Heaven: The Spiritual Roots of Rock- n-Roll.* New York: Ballantine Books, 1986.

Whitburn, Joel, edit. *The Billboard Book of Top 40 Hits.* New York: Billboard Publications, 1987.

White, Timothy. *Rock Lives.* New York: Holt & Co., 1990.